Flipping Housing

Secrets to Finding, Fixing and Flipping For Profit

This publication is designed to provide accurate and authoritative information in regard
 to the subject matter covered. It is sold with understanding that the publisher is not
 engaged in rendering legal, accounting, or other professional services. If legal advice
 or other expert advice is required, the services of a competent professional person
 should be sought.

Library of Congress Cataloging-in-Publication Data

Segal, Lloyd M.,

Flipping Houses;

ISBN-13: 978-1484015223

ISBN-10: 1484015223

   1. Flipping Houses – United States – Popular works. I. Title

c 2013 by Lloyd Segal
All rights reserved.
Printed in the Unites States of America

This publication may not be reproduced, stored in a retrieval system, or transmitted in
whole or in part, In any form or by any means, electronic, mechanical, photocopying,

recording, or otherwise, without the prior written of Regency Publication.

Printing number:

Cover Design: Deborah Razo, www.RAZD.com
Photographs: Dennis Finn (1943-2013)

Regency Books
PO Box 643065
Los Angeles, California 90064

Other books by Lloyd M. Segal:

Stop Foreclosure Now in California (Nolo)

Stop Foreclosure Now (AMACOM)

Foreclosure Investing (Regency)

Acknowledgements

I wanted to take this opportunity to especially thank those individuals who so graciously helped in the compiling, editing, and critiquing this book. Their suggestions and advice were warmly welcomed; Sam Sadat, Michael Scher, Ben Daidone, Bentley Radcliff, Bob Nirkind, Desiree Doubrox, Ginger Atherton, Janet Canas, Steve Maizes, Dennis Henson, Linda Pliagas, Deborah Razo, Kelly Morgan, Arnie Abramson, Tim Heritage, Barry Nathanson, , Christine Gilmore, Dan Ringwald, Geraldine Barry, Howard & Jeremy Gordon, Janet Canas, Ken Stirbl, Orlando Cruz, Ray Chagolla, Robert Keller, Scott Friedman, Robert Keller, Tom Todoroff, Geoffrey Thaw, Wynne Wallace, Michael Pasternak, Gary, Kelly, Murray, and Harold Segal, Ray Arthun, John Weisickle, Kurt and Cyndi Kramer.

I could not have completed this book without their help and encouragement!

About The Author

Trained as an attorney, Lloyd Segal is a mortgage banker, author, real estate investor, and public speaker. Now located in Santa Monica, California, Mr. Segal was born in Pittsburgh Pennsylvania. He graduated Boston University and Southwestern University School of Law School (where he was the President of the Student Bar Association), and studied International Law at the University of Innsbruck, Austria.

Lloyd is the author of *"Everything You Wanted to Know About Chapter 11 Bankruptcy...but Were Afraid to Ask,* and *"Stop Foreclosure Now in California" (published by Nolo Press, Berkeley, CA),* "*Stop Foreclosure Now"* (published by the American Management Association, New York, NY, and selected the *"Best Personal Finance Book of the Year"* by USA Book News), and *"Foreclosure Investing"* (published by Regency Books).

Lloyd is an informative public speaker with over 25 years of professional real estate experience as an investor, mortgage banker and real estate attorney. He has been interviewed and/or quoted on National Public Radio, CNN, Los Angeles Times, Parade Magazine, Smart Money, Publisher's Weekly, and numerous other radio, TV, and newspapers around the country. He is also a frequent guest speaker at universities, boards of realtors, Coldwell Banker national conventions, and numerous other real estate and service organizations throughout the United States.

Lloyd is the founder of the House Flipping Network, which provides in-depth educational services with respect to all aspects to finding, fixing and flipping properties.

Table of Contents

Introduction

Section A. **You**:		16
1.	Flipping houses is actually very easy.	17
2.	You don't need to be an expert to be a flipper.	19
3.	You can a full-time or part-time flipper.	21
4.	Flipping houses offers you many opportunities.	23
5.	Assemble a Dream Team to help you.	25
6.	Use partners whenever possible.	31
7.	Losing a deal is never a waste of your time.	35

Section B. **Homeowners**:		37
8.	Don't take unfair advantage of distressed homeowners.	38
9.	Understand why the homeowner is distressed.	40
10.	As a flipper, you can help distressed homeowners.	43
11.	Homeowners have no control over the foreclosure procedures.	46
12.	Don't feel guilty buying from distressed homeowners.	48
13.	Question what the homeowner tells you.	51
14.	If the former owners won't vacate, you should evict them.	53
15.	Pay the back taxes if they haven't already been paid.	58

Section C. **Houses**: 60
16. Look for houses to flip in all neighborhoods. 61
17. Just because a property is in foreclosure does not mean there is something wrong with it. 63
18. Always inspect the house. 65
19. Even if you can't get inside, you can still estimate a property's value. 68
20. Get an appraisal whenever possible. 72
21. Location, location, location. 78
22. Always do your homework before you buy. 81
23. Always get clear title to the property. 83
24. Distressed properties don't always need costly repairs. 89
25. Watch out for pre-existing problems. 93
26. Treat your neighbors good. 96

Section D. **Finding Properties**: 98
27. You don't need to be an insider to find deals. 99
28. It is never too early to find a good deal. 101
29. Foreclosure notices are great sources of deals. 103
30. The best deals are near you. 105
31. Buy the property directly from the homeowner prior to the auction. 108
32. There is always enough time to buy a foreclosure property. 113
33. Think outside the box. 116

Section E. **Realtors**: 119
  34. You don't need Realtors to find properties. 120
  35. Realtors don't have the best deals. 123
  36. You don't need Realtors to buy foreclosures properties. 125
  37. Sometimes you can find good deals through Realtors. 127

Section F. **Deals**: 130
  38. Regardless whether real estate is increasing or decreasing, there are always good deals. 131
  39. Structure your deals to make a reasonable profit. 134
  40. Besides the purchase price, there are other costs you must consider. 137
  41. You can find good deals in the Bankruptcy Courts. 140
  42. Bankruptcy properties are good deals. 143
  43. Not every property is a good deal. 147
  44. Consult with your dream team before buying. 151
  45. Don't let "buyer's panic" affect you .153

Section G. **Financing**: 155
  46. The house doesn't need to be in good condition to be financed. 156
  47. Never use all of your own money to buy houses. 159
  48. You don't need your own money to buy houses. 161

49.	Flip contracts (not houses).	163
50.	You can assume or take subject to the existing loan.	166
51.	Develop long term relationships with lenders.	169
52.	Lenders want to do business with you.	172
53.	Use hard money lenders when needed.	174
54.	Use your home equity loan to purchase properties.	178

Section H. **Auctions**: 182
55.	Foreclosure auctions are great for finding houses.	183
56.	Attend auctions and bid on houses.	187
57.	It doesn't matter how many people bid at the trustee's sale.	189
58.	You need a strategy when bidding at the auction.	192
59.	Avoid "buyer's panic" at the auction.	195
60.	Don't expect immediate possession after the auction.	198

Section I. **REOs**: 202
61.	REOs are a great source for houses.	203
62.	Buy REO properties directly from lenders.	208
63.	Government REOs are good deals.	215

Section J. **Rehabbing** 220
64.	Before you begin rehab, clean the house.	221
65.	Prepare a thorough "Scope of Work."	223
66.	Rehab with quality but less expensive items.	226

67.	Double-check estimates and bids for accuracy.	229
68.	Monitor your contractors closely.	231
69.	Confirm your contractors are insured.	233
70.	Peg payments to job completion milestones.	235
71.	Use retentions judicially.	238
72.	Don't over-improve the house.	240
73.	Don't make the repairs and renovations yourself unless You have the time and skills	245
74.	Give the house a final cleaning.	249

Section K. **Exit strategies**: 250
75.	Always have a contingency plan.	251
76.	It doesn't matter that the former owner couldn't sell the house.	254
77.	You can sell a house without completing renovations.	258
78.	Don't try to squeeze extra profits when you flip.	262
79.	Expect delays when flipping houses.	267
80.	Consider all of your strategies for each house.	269

Conclusion: 273
81.	Learning never stops.	274

Introduction

It took 20 years to write this book. Yes, 20 years! It evolved during hundreds of seminars, classes, courses, workshops, and boot camps I've conducted over the years on the subject of flipping houses. Thanks to my students, I cobbled together these secrets to flipping in response to their insightful questions.

Whenever I asked my students what was the most difficult aspect to real estate investing in general, and flipping houses specifically, they consistently referred to *"getting started."* They didn't know what to do first, where to go, who to talk to, or what to say. In other words, getting started presented the most difficulty for them. As I analyzed the consistency of the questions and their interest at my explanations, I realized that the answers to each of their questions was a *"secret,"* a kernel of knowledge that would shed light on a previously unknown, but alluring world. I also realized that the secrets fell into easily identifiable categories; homeowners, you (the investor), houses, finding properties, deals, financing, realtors, trustee's sales, REOs, rehabbing, and exit strategies. I also discovered that if I could answer their questions with concise straightforward explanations (i.e. secrets) that they could easily understand, they would remember them and feel more comfortable getting started.

Thus, this book evolved, rather than was written. First ten secrets. Then 32 secrets, which quickly expanded to 76, and then 86, and then suddenly 93, with no end in sight! I couldn't stop myself! Eventually, I stopped writing and began the arduous process of whittling the secrets down to a more manageable number. 80 was ultimately the magic number.

Belatedly I added a "half" secret, so to speak. But how can you have a half secret, you ask? It is a half secret because it is slightly different than the other secrets. Also, because a half secret creates curiosity, doesn't it? But before we proceed, you need to promise me you won't spoil the surprise and jump to the end of the book to read the half secret. Promise? After all, it's at the end of the book for a reason. Please wait until you've read all of the other secrets first before peeking. Think of it as dessert. Something sweet after all of those savory courses are finished.

What I also found is that if I kept my responses (secrets) brief, the students paid closer attention to them. So even though each of the secrets is deserving of an entire chapter, each one has been edited down to no more than one to three pages in length. Imagine if I hadn't; 80 ½ chapters! It would have been a very thick book! Indeed, one that very few people would have read. So this book accomplishes the task much more effectively. I hope you will agree.

In "Flipping Houses," I've attempted to demystify the flipping process. I've given secrets on how to find properties, how to rehab them, and how to sell them. Whether you're a first time homebuyer, or an experienced investor, learning these secrets will save you hours of time, thousands of dollars, and avoid countless mistakes.

In this book, I've shared the secrets and many opportunities. I've also shared plenty of useful information on how to find good deals, how to conduct due diligence, and how to create an exit strategy to assure yourself a profit.

As you read this book, keep in mind that regardless of whether real estate is going through an up or down market, there are always properties available for you to flip. You can take advantage of the situation and purchase houses substantially below market value. And it doesn't matter whether you've never bought real estate before or know how to rehab a house, these secrets will guide you down the path to successful flipping.

Keep in mind, flipping houses is profitable, but it's also risky. There is no guaranty of profits, and you could lose money. But every good investment has risks. In this book, I'll help put those risks and profits into perspective, as I disclose secrets to minimize your risks and maximize your profits. But don't get me wrong, it is not easy. If it were easy everyone would do it! It takes work. But if you're willing to do the work, I'll share with you the secrets of successful flipping. And if you use these secrets, you will be successful. So read on with the confidence that you'll be learning secrets to flipping that most real estate veterans never share, and most novice investors never know. As the saying goes, knowledge is power. The knowledge you will gain by reading this book will empower you to flip with confidence.

Now shhh! I'm about to tell you some secrets...

Section A: You

Secret 1

Flipping Houses Is Actually Very Easy

Taking on new challenges can be stressful and scary. But don't let those emotions cause you to think flipping houses is too complicated, because it's not! The rules and regulations governing flipping are straightforward and understandable. And although at first the learning curve will be a little steep, it smooth out the longer you do it. Flipping is simply a process, and any process can be learned. Real estate investors come from all walks of life and educational backgrounds. Regardless of your background or education, you will be able to learn this process. In fact, there are no special qualifications for being a flipper. You can do this!

Remember how you felt when you first learned to drive an automobile? Very complicated right? Yet driving is probably second nature to you now. Well, the same with flipping. Eventually, with a little practice, buying and selling houses will become as second-nature as driving a car. Keep at it; keep practicing. It will get easier.

It only seems complicated now because you're just starting out. Successful flipping takes time and experience. More importantly, it takes motivation, drive, determination, and hard work. You can overcome inexperience by doing your homework, asking for guidance, and working hard. Stick with it and soon you'll be experienced and won't think of it as complicated.

If you're still scared, here's some good news! A built-in safety net exists to help you, right where you live. Real estate professionals are in business to help people just like you. For example, real estate agents need you. They need homes to sell or they don't earn commissions. Lenders need you. They need to loan their funds so that they can earn interest. Contractors need you. Title companies need you. Attorneys need you. You'll need to form a "Dream Team" of these professionals to help you. Your dream team will welcome your calls and your questions. You'll build long-term business relationships with your team members, and they with you. And as you become more experienced, you will pass on the wisdom you've gained to others who can benefit from the path you've chosen.

Secret 2
You Don't Need to be an Expert to Be a Flipper

Finding deals, negotiating with homeowners and Realtors, bidding at trustee's sales, and repairing and flipping homes is not rocket science. Thousands of Americans do it every day without specialized knowledge or training. Many people buy and sell dozens of properties each year. The only difference between you and those flippers is experience and effort. Before they flipped their first house, they didn't have experience either!

Buying and selling properties is not a get-rich-quick scheme. It's also not easy. It takes time, dedication, and real effort on your part to succeed. If you don't put in the effort, you won't succeed.

Now that I think about it, successful flippers share some common traits. They treat flipping as a business, objectively analyzing each deal for its risk and reward. They communicate effectively. They express themselves clearly so others understand their requirements, goals, and intentions. They respect distressed homeowners and attempt to preserve dignity in the relationship. They seek win-win situations with homeowners and lenders. They build long-term business relationships with contractors, real estate agents, escrow officers, mortgage brokers, and other professionals. And finally, they demonstrate a real commitment to success. They're willing to work hard, to overcome problems, and to stick to their plans and their goals even when times are tough.

So, you see, you don't need to be an expert. Experience is helpful, but effort and dedication are crucial. No amount of knowledge will help you if you're not willing to put in the time and effort required to succeed. This is true of anything that is worthwhile and profitable. After all, almost flipper has lost money on one or more transactions, even experienced flippers. What makes these flippers successful is that they learn from their mistakes and the mistakes of others. They learned how to string together more successes than failures. To minimize your risk, start with one property at a time and build in enough buffer (20% or more) so you won't lose your shirt. Eventually, as you gain experience, you'll flip more properties.

Secret 3

You Can Be a Full-time or Part-time Flipper

The beauty of flipping is that you don't have to do it full-time. You can do it part-time. Look around you. Most people who buy and sell residential rental properties do so "on the side." They don't do it full-time. We all know people with full-time jobs who own several properties. Right? They buy one house at a time to repair, renovate, and then flip, doing some of the work themselves at night (or on weekends) and hiring friends or contractors to perform any necessary skilled labor. Still other investors create partnerships: One partner finds and evaluates the deals and lines-up funding and financing, while the other takes care of the repairs and renovations.

In fact, finding a partner or partners is a great way to spread the workload and at the same time minimize each partner's risk. (And working as a team can be a lot of fun!)

If you already have a full-time job, you're under no pressure to make a living from flipping. You can move at your own pace and your own comfort level. But if your comfort level is currently low, then working with a partner is a great idea. If you do decide to partner with another investor, be as careful in choosing your new partner as you are when choosing a mate. This doesn't necessarily mean that your partnership will be without problems (after all, half of all marriages in the United States end in divorce), but it does decrease your chances of taking on a partner who's not committed to carrying his share of the workload.

Flipping houses offers a variety of moneymaking opportunities, both full-time and part-time. With flipping, you can find an undervalued property and flip it for a quick profit. Or, you can rehab it and then sell it for an even greater profit.

Secret 4

Flipping Offers You Many Opportunities

When choosing a career path, each of us must decide what is most important and act accordingly. Choose the path that's right for you and follow it. The last thing any of us wants to do is to look back and wish we had chosen a different path.

Let's say you're an manager working for a large corporation. You make $85,000 per year. Why did you choose this job? Hopefully it's because you enjoy the work and you feel the pay and benefits are appropriate for your talents, background, and experience.

Now say you have been flipping properties in your spare time. Over the last three years, you've bought and sold four properties per year for an average profit of $20,000. You have grown confident in your ability to spot good opportunities, make cost-effective repairs and renovations, and flip the house for a reasonable profit. You've also found good people to work with: your lender, real estate agents, title company, attorney, and a few key contractors you can count on. Should you keep your full-time job or take the plunge and become a full-time flipper?

Well, it depends on you. What do you enjoy doing the most? If you enjoy flipping properties and feel you can replace your full-time income by handling three or four more deals each year, why wouldn't you? If you feel you could put more money in your pocket by handling five or six more flips (and again, you enjoy the work), so much the better. So if you enjoy flipping and you can earn more, why not?

At the same time, everyone's path is different. Some investors enjoy doing just two or three flips a year. They are content. They may feel taking on any more deals would create too much pressure and too many demands on their time. Other investors like the security of keeping a full-time job. In their case, security is more important than the potential for higher income.

When you're trying to decide whether to take the leap and become a full-time flipper, don't forget to account for any additional benefits you may be receiving with your full-time job, including health insurance, paid vacations, retirement, and health insurance. All those things taken together can represent a good chunk of change.

In the end, no one has the answers except you. After balancing all of the factors, choose the path that is right for you and follow it.

Secret 5

Assemble a Dream Team to Help You

You can do this alone, but why would you. How many people do you know who succeed entirely on their own? I bet not many. That's because we all need people along the way to help us. So you need to form your own *"Dream Team"* of real estate professionals to help you. After all, building a team dramatically increases your chances for success. Plus, with the right team in place you can handle more opportunities and generate additional revenue to more than cover the expense of having other people helping you.

With flipping, you don't have to be an expert. But it will be helpful to your success if you have experts on your side. Let's look at how you can build a top-notch "Dream Team" of real estate professionals to help you. Your Dream Team should include a real estate agent, mortgage broker, escrow officer, general contractor, title company, home inspector, and attorney. Each of these professionals makes a living providing services to people like you, so they'll want to be on your team.

Real Estate Agent. An agent will help you flip the houses you buy. They will also provide you with sales comparables ("comps") for properties you're considering and inside information about the neighborhood, the area, and the real estate market. A real estate agent is licensed by the state and a member of the National Association of Realtors, which confers the designation of "realtor." They can also be instrumental in recommending other possible candidates for your Dream Team.

Mortgage Broker. Mortgage brokers help you secure financing. A good
mortgage broker/loan officer is state licensed, and a member of the National Association of Mortgage Brokers (NAMB) and/or the Mortgage Brokers Association (MBA). He has at least five years experience, and has earned professional designations. He understands flipping and can help you borrow on the *"After-Repaired Value"* of the property, not just on the purchase price. (The after repaired value is the market value of a property after it has been rehabbed.) By sourcing funds based on the future value, you'll have access to more capital to pay for repairs and renovations. He has earned positive references from past clients as well as from industry professionals, including real estate agents and title companies.

Home Inspector. A licensed home inspector evaluates the quality and condition of a house. If you purchase a distressed property, you often agree to purchase the property *"as is."* So when you purchase from the homeowner, you can have your home inspector conduct the inspection and make the sale conditional on the house passing inspection. Here are some of the items home inspectors evaluate: structure, foundation, exterior, roofing, windows, siding, plumbing, electrical, heating, air-conditioning, and fireplaces. Home inspectors check the condition of each item and provide a report summarizing their findings. To find a good home inspector, ask your real estate agent, and other members of your dream team for referrals. Another excellent way to find licensed home inspectors in your area is through the American Society of Home Inspectors. Visit their website at www.ASHI.com, and enter your ZIP code in the "*Find a Home Inspector*" box. Such a person not only can point out problems but also can give you a rough estimate of how much it will cost to fix.

Title Insurance Company. The primary purpose of a title insurance company is to insure legal conveyance of the property's title and encumbrances. The title company takes care of the paperwork and legalities of completing a title transfer, such as deeds, mortgages, and deeds of trust. But a title company does so much more that they are an invaluable member of your Dream Team. Title companies conduct research of the property's history and insure there are no existing problems with the property's title. Most importantly, they will issue a Property Profile (at no cost) or a Preliminary Title Report (small cost) which will give you a complete picture of liens recorded against the property and whether they will insure your purchase. The title company you choose should understand the flipping process, because they will know what common problems to look for in the title history and how to clear them.

Escrow. Escrow is a neutral third party that is responsible for handling real estate transactions. Now, not all transactions involve an escrow. For example, when you purchase directly from a homeowner, there may be no time for an escrow. However, when you purchase short sales, probates, REO properties, or standard transactions, you will need an escrow. During those transactions, it will be invaluable for you to have an experienced escrow officer that knows the ins-and-outs of the transaction and will keep you well-informed.

Contractor. A general contractor is an individual (or a company) hired to work on repairs and/or renovations of a house. The general contractor typically employs or hires subcontractors who specialize in areas like plumbing, electrical work, carpentry, tile work, and so forth. When you buy a property, it may need repair or renovation ("rehab"). You might need someone to install new plumbing, electrical wiring, flooring, or windows, or to repair the roof. A contractor can handle these tasks for you. Unless the repairs or renovations needed are extensive, you can serve as the general contractor, hiring subcontractors to help you. But if you're unsure about your construction abilities, or the time you'll have available, considering hiring a general contractor. Time is money. Get recommendations from your real estate agent, mortgage brokers, and other real estate investors to find honest and reliable contractors.

Attorney. Attorneys are specialists, and some specialize in real estate. Make sure you work with an attorney that specializes in real estate law, particularly transactions. Ask your real estate agent and mortgage broker for recommendations or call the local bar association and ask for the names and phone numbers of attorneys who specializes in real estate. Look for an attorney who is responsive, who returns your calls promptly, and who seems interested in working with you. Flipping often happens quickly, and your attorney must be able to respond quickly as well.

Partners. While we're on the subject of building a dream team, let's talk about partners. A good partner can help you achieve more than you could ever achieve on your own. (Of course, a bad partner can make your life a nightmare!). Nevertheless, if you decide to create a partnership, pick someone whose talents and abilities complement yours. For example, if you aren't comfortable directing contractors, consider bringing in a partner to oversee property repairs and renovations. You may be great at evaluating properties and arranging financing, and your partner may excel at managing repairs and renovations. If you do create a partnership, have your attorney draft a contract detailing your responsibilities and your business arrangement. But whatever you do, don't work on a handshake basis. If things go badly, your partnership agreement will help minimize the damage. If you do partner-up with someone, make sure you both have control of the money. You should also both be required to sign any checks to pay for repairs and renovations. Neither party should blindly trust the other when it comes to matters of money. You should both be in the know and share decisions on how that money is spent. Resolving those issues upfront should help you avoid unforeseeable problems in the future.

Secret 6

Use Partners Whenever Possible

Sure, you may lower your profits, but with a partner, you'll also lower your risk. More importantly, you will increase your leverage.

Many people avoid partnerships because they don't want to give-up control, share profits, or fear their partner won't do anything. But that's a short-sighted view. Partners are invaluable in flipping. They share responsibilities, risk, and profits. In fact, a good partner can help keep you motivated and focused, and keep you from feeling alone when times get tough.

Most importantly, partners are valuable when you need money and/or financing. Assuming you can't buy a house on your own, a partner can bring cash into the deal or qualify for financing. Or your partner can pay for the repairs and renovations that you otherwise couldn't afford to make. Finding a partner with ready cash can make all the difference. You may end-up sharing the profits, but that's better than letting the deal slip away and making no money!

When two or more persons go into business together, they usually form
a partnership. Among the advantages, it's fairly easy to set-up a partnership and doesn't cost much in the way of attorney's fees. Also, there is the division of equipment, supplies, and labor.

The major disadvantage is the possibility of disagreements later down the road. Usually these disagreements involve money and/or responsibilities. But there are ways to protect yourself (and your partner) if those situations arise.

If you're considering a partnership, discuss the following issues with your partner(s): How much money will each partner contribute? Will the property be owned 50/50 or in some other percentage? Who will be liable on the loan? Will you carry equal workloads? If not, how will you divide the work and responsibilities? Will profits be distributed equally? When will the property be sold? Who has the final say in case there is a disagreement? What happens in the event of illness, disability, or death of a partner?

If you decide to form a partnership, make sure you create a comprehensive written agreement. The more complete your agreement, the fewer disagreements you'll have later on. The first step is discussing and then writing down everything pertaining to your partnership. Put everything in writing. And I do mean EVERYTHING! Don't go into the partnership assuming you'll be able to work out any problems if they come up. When things get sticky, you probably won't be amenable to resolving your differences.

Most importantly, assume in your partnership agreement that the worst might happen. Include a clause providing for how disputes will be resolved. If your prospective partner objects to putting together a detailed agreement, find another partner.

When forming a partnership, everyone usually has stars in their eyes about how much money they're going to make together. But when significant problems arise and force the abrupt termination of the partnership, the partners frequently don't have an "exit strategy." They are so upset with one another they cannot agree upon a fair and equitable breakup. So, Rule #1, have an exit strategy in place from day one. Your partnership agreement should incorporate your exit strategy and how the profit, expenses, and properties will be distributed upon termination. In other words, how will you divide partnership-owned assets should you and your partners decide to split-up?

After you've written up your agreement, give it to an attorney. The attorney will then draft a formal agreement for preliminary approval by all partners. After corrections, additions, and deletions, the attorney will draft the final agreement for you and your partners' signatures. The agreement should make provisions for division of responsibilities, obligations, expenditures, profits, losses, assets, liabilities, and exit strategies, as well as long-term illness, disability, or death of a partner. In this way, you'll be assured of a successful partnership. And, in the unlikely event of disagreement, you'll have a written exit strategy you can follow.

Secret 7
<u>Losing a Deal is Never a Waste of Your Time</u>

If a distressed homeowner doesn't want to sell his home, good for him! You may have missed a good flip, but he was able to keep his cherished home. It's hard to be too disappointed if you think of it that way.

But the reality is that less than 10% of distressed homeowners are able to save their homes. Most homeowners can't stop the foreclosure and ultimately lose their homes. After all, borrowers who can't make their monthly payments are unlikely to suddenly find the funds necessary to reinstate their loans.

Let's say, for the sake of argument, you're in one of those rare situations where after extensive negotiations, the homeowner you've been negotiating with won't sell to you on your terms. What happens to you? Well, you worked hard to evaluate the deal. You did your due diligence (i.e. analyzed the terms, scrutinized the sale comparables in the neighborhood, estimated potential repair costs, studied what you could flip the house for, and arranged financing). You've put in your usual professional effort to make it happen. Nevertheless, the homeowners decided not to sell to you because your offer wasn't good enough for him. Well, you're out some time (and time is money), but look what you've gained.

You've gained invaluable experience. Every property you evaluate increases your experience level as a flipper. You developed a stronger rapport with your dream team of professionals and you learned lessons you can apply down the road with other deals. You see, you can and will learn something new from every situation, every deal, and every property. And because this is really a "people business" you will also learn something from every seller you meet. In other words, think of every deal (even the ones that don't happen), as a classroom that provides valuable, real-world training you'll never get in a school.

As you can now see, a lost deal is never a waste of time or money. It is an opportunity to learn and become a better investor.

Here's another secret: If you've been working with a homeowner in foreclosure who ultimately save their home, send them a card or letter congratulating them. In that way, if they end-up in trouble later and need to sell their home, they'll remember your kindness and call you first. Plus, they'll refer you to their friends, family, and neighbors if they should suddenly need to sell their homes.

Section B: Homeowners

Secret 8

Don't Take Unfair Advantage of Distressed Homeowners

You need to understand the homeowner's predicament. They are in the process of losing their home. By the time they've contacted you, they have missed several mortgage payments, received foreclosure notices, and exhausted all of their options. They probably discussed a loan modification with their lender, but without success. They probably talked to a realtor about selling their home, but found out there wasn't enough time, or that in its present condition probably wouldn't sell for much. They might have talked to a mortgage broker about refinancing, but found out they didn't have enough equity or didn't qualify. They may have also discussed filing bankruptcy with an attorney, but discovered that was a bad idea.

So before they called you, they probably came to the conclusion that their only viable solution is to sell their home or they'll lose everything. At the foreclosure sale, they will lose ownership of their home, and eventually they will be evicted (if they don't voluntarily move). Worse, not only will they lose their home, the foreclosure will affect their credit for seven years and make it nearly impossible for them to buy another house or rent an apartment. So their situation is truly dire. It's that simple, and it's not your fault. Their only viable alternative is to sell their home, and sell it quickly.

They may even have talked to other investors and found they weren't offering very good deals. Now it is your opportunity. So while the circumstances are unfortunate for the homeowners, you, as a flipper, can provide the homeowners with a graceful exit.

Under these circumstances, always treat the homeowners with dignity and respect. Even though you're going to rehab and flip the house for profit, don't take advantage of these people. Be fair in the transaction. Have empathy and compassion for their predicament. Explain everything, disclose everything, and put all of your understandings in writing. In addition to making the homeowners feel better about what's happening, it will improve your reputation and help convince other distressed homeowners to call you (instead of someone else) when they need to sell their home.

Secret 9

Understand Why the Homeowner is Distressed

Some of the best candidates for flipping are distressed houses. But behind every distressed house there is a distressed homeowner that you need to understand. If a family loses their home, it's easy to assume they were financially irresponsible or got in over their heads. Despite the fact that those are possible reasons for foreclosure, more often foreclosure is out of the homeowner's control. Defaulting on a loan could also have been caused by:

Unemployment. Losing a job is the most common cause of foreclosure. As the unemployment rates increases, foreclosure rates naturally rise. When the family loses income, mortgage payments are understandably seen as less important (in the short term) to putting food on the table. But even during booming economic times, some companies layoff employees, transfer or consolidate, or just plain go out of business.

Medical Problems. Unexpected illnesses or injuries can cost families thousands in medical bills. Worse, the high rate of uninsured Americans (before the health reform bill takes affect) leaves fewer families with a safety net to cover those costs. When a medical emergency occurs, mortgage payments are sometimes understandably seen as less important.

Divorce. Approximately half of all marriages end in divorce. Who keeps the house and who pays for the house, can be major issues. Often, the house is not even affordable anymore. Unfortunately, in many instances, pure spite takes over and common sense disappears! The first casualty is often the mortgage payment.

Adjustable Rate Mortgages. If the borrowers took out adjustable rate mortgages, the interest rate eventually readjusts. The unfortunate side of that equation is that those interest rates may increase and the payments rise. As a result, homeowners with fixed incomes may find themselves unable to afford the higher payments and default.

Death. If the sole wage-earner dies and the family loses that income, the likelihood increases that the family will lose their home in foreclosure.

Taxes. Some mortgage payments do not include tax escrow accounts, and it becomes easy for homeowners to fall behind in their taxes. In these cases, the lender can call the loan due and accelerate the payments to avoid a tax lien sale.

Increased cost of living. When salary increases fail to keep pace with inflation, homeowners may not be able to maintain their lifestyle. I have seen sudden increases in property taxes, insurance premiums, and fuel costs without comparable increases in personal income.

Predatory Lending. Irresponsible, greedy, or poorly-trained loan officers sold homeowners on sub-prime or exotic loans that set them up for failure.

So you see, there are many reasons people fall behind with their mortgage payments, not always related to financial irresponsibility. Sadly, bad things do happen to well-meaning, financially responsible people. So when dealing with distressed homeowners, avoid making judgments or placing blame. Move them beyond the past. The homeowners need to stop beating themselves up or blaming others for their misfortune. The homeowners need to focus on their future which means selling their home (to you) and renting/buying a less expensive home.

Secret 10

As a Flipper, You Can Help Distressed Homeowners

Imagine for a moment you are a homeowner in foreclosure or on the verge of foreclosure. You don't know what to do, who to trust, or where to turn. You have no idea where to find the money to bring your loan current. Your credit is already trashed and will get worse if the foreclosure sale occurs. Your home has serious deferred maintenance and you don't have the money to fix it. Nobody wants to buy your property in its present condition, nor will any lenders refinance it. If the foreclosure sale is conducted, you will lose all of your equity (if you have any), and your home. You are desperate and don't know what to do. So in a panic you move out and abandon your home. Heartbreaking scenario isn't it?

How can you help? Easy. You are a flipper. You understand the homeowner's predicament. You can assist these distressed homeowners in any number of ways. You can explore options they have, including negotiating with the foreclosing lender, selling their home, refinancing, obtaining another loan, filing a lawsuit, or filing bankruptcy. You can also encourage them to take action before they run out of time.

If they ultimately decide to sell their home to you, you can help them maintain their dignity and what's left of their credit. If they have any positive equity remaining in their property, you can offer them some cash. Remember, their equity will be wiped-out if the foreclosure sale occurs, so anything they receive from you will be "found" money. On the other hand, if they have negative equity (meaning their loan balance exceeds the value of their home), you can negotiate a short sale with their lender. In that way, the property can be sold to you and the homeowners won't have to pay the shortage. (With a short sale, the lender agrees to accept a partial payment of the total balance owed as payment in full.)

You may notice that a couple of these options could result in you not buying the house. But that's okay, because in order to act with integrity, you must accept the fact that you may not always get the deal. Sometimes just helping people should be your priority. So always do the right thing. Ideally, you want to create win-win situations; situations in which the homeowner rids themselves of an unwanted house and you buy a property below market that you can rehab and flip. But if that's not possible, help the homeowner anyway.

Buying from distressed homeowners also offers advantages to you, rather than waiting for the foreclosure sale. You (and your contractors) will have a chance to inspect the house thoroughly, so you'll know exactly what condition the house is in. Also, the homeowner will more likely leave the house in good condition, as opposed to after a foreclosure auction.

Keep in mind, helping a homeowner in distress should never involve taking advantage of that person. Act with integrity and professionalism at all times. If you can develop a win-win situation, it will be the best for both the homeowner and you. You'll make a good deal, and the homeowner will refer you to their family, friends, and neighbors (who may also be eager to sell their properties).

Secret 11

Homeowners Have No Control Over the Foreclosure Procedures

If you find a property that is already in foreclosure, you'll need to consider the homeowner's predicament. Once the foreclosure process is underway, only the lender can cancel the foreclosure sale, not the homeowner. There are only a few things the homeowner can do to stop the foreclosure. The homeowner can either bring the loan current (which is unlikely), file bankruptcy, or sell the property (hopefully to you),

Keep in mind, the lender does not want to foreclose. They don't want the house. They're in the business of lending money, not selling real estate. Banks aren't permitted to make a profit on real estate sales. In fact, banks operate under federal regulations prohibiting them from being in the business of selling real estate. Instead, banks want a predictable stream of mortgage payments. They don't want the hassles and headaches involved in foreclosing a property, renovating it, and then selling it as an REO. But if the homeowner is non-responsive, they have no other recourse; they will foreclose.

Aside from bringing payments current or selling the house, the only other way the homeowner can stop the foreclosure is by declaring bankruptcy. As soon as the homeowners files, the Court issues an *"Automatic Stay"* (i.e. injunction) which basically freezes everything, including the foreclosure. Creditors (including the foreclosing lender) then file motions in court to have the automatic stay lifted (released). If the court lifts the automatic stay, then the foreclosing lender can proceed with the foreclosure. So ultimately, nothing has been gained. Bankruptcy used to be good idea for homeowners because this process took one to two years. It was though the home was lost indefinitely in purgatory. But with the new bankruptcy laws and the fast-track process, the automatic stay lasts no more than one to two months. So bankruptcy is no longer the panacea for homeowners it used to be.

Besides, if foreclosure is a bad situation for a homeowner; bankruptcy is even worse! In foreclosure, only the house is lost. In bankruptcy, other assets besides the house may also be lost to satisfy creditors. However, for some homeowners, particularly those buried in unsecured debt (such as credit card debt), bankruptcy could be their last and best option.

Secret 12

Don't Feel Guilty Buying From Distressed Homeowners

Foreclosure properties are some of the best candidates for flipping. But many flippers avoid foreclosure properties because they feel they are taking advantage of distressed homeowners. That's an understandable emotion because none of us wants to profit from the hardship of others. Nevertheless, you shouldn't feel guilty and here's why.

Foreclosure laws and procedures exist to protect homeowners, not to harm them. These laws give homeowners extra time to find ways to overcome their financial difficulties and save their homes. By the time they've contacted you, they've probably exhausted most of those options. So your involvement is like throwing a lifesaver to someone that is drowning. In fact, the homeowners will see you as a financial savior if you buy their home during foreclosure.

Here's another secret: Homeowners who cannot reinstate their loans during foreclosure will inevitably lose their home no matter what you do. So if you don't buy the property from the homeowner, someone else will at the foreclosure auction or from the lender (called an "REO").

So either way, they will eventually lose their home. Plus, in non-judicial states, there are no post-sale redemption rights. This means that after the foreclosure auction, the homeowners won't get their home back.

As you can see, you are simply playing the role of purchasing a property that the homeowners can no longer afford. In fact, flippers like you are an integral part of the real estate financing process. Lenders need to sell foreclosure properties before, during, and after the foreclosure auction. These lenders are repaid by the sale proceeds. So while foreclosure is certainly an unfortunate outcome for homeowners, it is necessary to ensure the stability of the financial institutions that make loans to homeowners, and the health of other creditors, contractors, and real estate professionals.

While we're at it, here are some things you should never do:

    1. Withhold information from the homeowners that could help them sell the house themselves (and save some of their equity in the property).

    2. Mislead homeowners into thinking their only option is to sell to you.

    3. Befriend the homeowners so they'll sell the property to you (even though doing so is not in their best interest).

4. Buy a house at the foreclosure auction and then tell the homeowners they have to move out immediately, even though you're required to give them a 3-Day Notice to Quit, and then follow formal eviction procedures.

If you question what you're saying to homeowners may not in their best interest, in all likelihood you're doing something wrong. While you want to make a profit when you flip the house, you don't want to misrepresent facts. Always present yourself professionally, act in good faith, uphold the highest ethical standards, and follow the laws of your state. Most importantly, always treat homeowners with compassion, fairness, and respect. If you do, you will be helping someone recover from a terrible situation.

Secret 13

Question What the Homeowner Tells You

The best houses for flipping are owned by distressed homeowners who are either in default, or worse, in foreclosure. So let's understand the predicament homeowners are in. Distressed homeowners are emotionally fragile. They're in a desperate situation. They are not only losing the biggest purchase of their lives, but also the home where they created family memories. If you take a step back and consider the situation objectively, it's understandable why homeowners may bend the truth on occasion in order to sell their home. As a flipper, you should be compassionate, but don't be gullible.

For example, some of their claims will be easy to verify. If a homeowner claims the house is in great shape, simply say, *"Great, then the inspection will be a breeze."* If they object to an inspection, that should raise a red flag.

Other homeowners are so desperate they'll say almost anything to convince you to let them stay in the home (while you rehab), or pay them money. They'll tell you their house is in perfect condition, or they have money coming in soon and will catch up on the payments, or they'll move out in a week (or as soon as they find a place to live), or they'll play on your emotions and claim that someone close to them is ill (or has recently passed away).

If you hear these stories, be sure to confirm any claims or excuses that sound fishy or odd. Once they have been verified, offer a suitable concession if you feel it's appropriate. Have the homeowners agree to that concession in writing, and then hold them to their agreements.

Here's another secret: Record any conversations you have with homeowners. But first ask the homeowners, for their protection (and yours), for permission to record your conversations. Also make sure you record yourself asking their permission and them giving permission. By recording your conversations, you'll have an audio record of exactly what you told the homeowners and what they told you, just in case disagreements ever arise in the future as to what was said in the past.

Secret 14

If the Former Owners Won't Vacate, You Should Evict Them

Once you've purchased a house from a homeowner or at the foreclosure auction, you are the legal owner. The former homeowners no longer have any right to possession. Most homeowners have already vacated by this time, while a few may remain. As the new owner, you are entitled to possession and it's now your responsibility to deal with the remaining occupants.

I recommend you do everything possible to work with the homeowners and encourage them to vacate voluntarily. For example, offer them incentives to help them vacate as quickly as possible. Do you have to offer help? Legally; no. But put yourself in their shoes. How would you feel if the situation were reversed?

Some will still not leave, no matter what you do. That's when you need to utilize the legal system. First serve the former homeowners with a *"3-Day Notice to Quit."* They then have three days to vacate.

If they don't, you will need to file a eviction lawsuit against them (which is called an *"unlawful detainer"*). You can handle the eviction process yourself, but I recommend getting the help of an attorney. In fact, find an attorney that specializes in eviction cases. See it as insurance. You may spend a little extra on attorney's fees, but you save thousands on unexpected legal issues.

File the eviction papers at the local courthouse. Make sure you make copies of important documents, including your purchase agreement or deed, and any other documents pertaining to the sale. You'll be assigned a court date, and a judge will hear the case.

The case will go to trial within 4-6 weeks depending on your local courthouse's calendar. Unless the homeowners successfully provide a legal reason why they need more time, the judge will typically grant judgment in your favor and issue a writ of possession.

Once the court has officially ruled in your favor, most former homeowners will comply and voluntarily vacate. But for those that don't, you'll have to contact the sheriff and have the homeowners evicted. The sheriff will go to the house and order the former homeowners to remove their belongings, or if they're not home, stand-by as your locksmith changes the locks.

As you can see, eviction is no fun. Not for you, and not for the people being evicted. When a sheriff forcibly evicts a family, their belongings are locked inside the house, or sometimes left out in the street. Neighbors usually come out to watch and may even pick through the belongings as if they were free for the taking. It is usually very humiliating for the family.

But whatever you do, don't attempt to forcibly evict the former homeowners on your own. You can never be sure what will happen. They could become angry or even violent, neighbors could try to walk off with some of the family's belongings, or the homeowners could try to accuse you of wrongdoing. Always call the sheriff. With the sheriff on the scene, you have someone who can keep the peace and act as a witness that you did nothing wrong.

While an unlawful detainer will ultimately solve the problem, try to avoid lawsuits if possible. Some homeowners take their frustration out on the property. And your insurance policy may cover the damage, but it will still take time and effort to repair the property before you can flip it. As an alternative to eviction proceedings, help the homeowners move out peaceably by:

Providing extra time: Some homeowners may have legitimate reasons why moving out immediately is difficult; illness, death in the family, children in school, or some other circumstance. If you wish, you can give them more time and negotiate a date certain when they will move out. But make sure you create a formal document stating that commitment, and have them sign it.

Providing a moving van: If the homeowners claim they don't have the funds to hire a moving company, consider renting a moving van for them. Your goal is to remove as many objections or issues as you can. After all, the sooner they're out, the sooner you can rehab the house.

Providing a dumpster: You can help the homeowners clean-up by providing a free dumpster (or roll-off container). Doing so may keep you from having to throw their trash and unwanted items away yourself after they leave.

Providing free storage: Some homeowners will claim they have nowhere to put their belongings. You can prepay for storage space for a few months, but don't enter into an open-ended agreement. You don't want to be stuck paying their bill for years to come.

Providing cash: Distressed homeowners are by definition suffering financial hardship and may not have the funds to make a deposit on an apartment or hire a moving van. You can offer them some money to help them out. However, instead of providing the funds up-front, make your agreement with them conditional upon them moving out on a specified date and leaving the premises clean and in good repair.

As you can see, working with the former homeowners to leave voluntarily is always advisable to initiating eviction through the courts. It is better for the homeowners, better for you, and certainly better for the property. So whenever possible go this route.

Secret 15

Pay the Back Taxes If They Haven't Already Been Paid

If you purchase a property from the homeowner while they are default , unpaid property taxes are problematic. While legally the responsibility of the homeowner, they typically don't have the money to pay them. After all, if they haven't paid the mortgage, they certainly haven't paid the taxes. In essence, their tax problem becomes your problem if the taxes are not paid. So either the homeowner agrees to pay the delinquent taxes as part of your deal, or you pay the taxes and deduct it from the monies you would otherwise paid the homeowner.

If you buy at the foreclosure auction, the delinquent taxes will likely be included in the amount you will pay in order to acquire the house.

REO properties are different. Lenders are concerned about taxes because taxes always take priority over all other liens (including the lender's deed of trust or mortgage). So in order to have clear title, the REO lender will typically pay the taxes and keep them current. In that event, if you're buying an REO from the lender, you will not pay any back taxes.

Secret 16

Look for Distressed Properties in All Neighborhoods

While "bad" neighborhoods have their share of troubled properties, you can also find distressed properties in good neighborhoods. In other words, if the homeowners cannot meet their obligations, distressed properties can be found in any neighborhood.

Distressed homeowners can be found anywhere, and in any neighborhood, due to any number of causes. For example, studies show that a loan's default risk is directly tied to the size of the down payment (and not the neighborhood). The lower the down payment, the greater the likelihood of default. And low down payments can be made on any property in any neighborhood, regardless of value. In cases where higher down payments were originally made, low interest rates make home equity loans and cash-out refinancing appealing, and caused homeowners to take out cash generated from appreciation.

Economic downturns cause foreclosure rates to increase, every day, in every city and county in the United States. As a result, families are in danger of losing their homes. This opens the door for you! But avoid the temptation to buy into an area with plenty of foreclosure properties just because finding foreclosures is easier. In areas where foreclosures are rampant, you may have trouble flipping the house later, after you finished the rehab. Ideally, you want to find the hidden gem -- a distressed house in a popular area.

The Census Bureau estimated that over the past ten years, billions in home equity was extracted through refinancing, taking out second mortgages, or accessing home equity lines of credit. The less equity remaining in a home, the less cushion the homeowner has, and the higher the likelihood of default. When cash-out extractions rise, more homeowners are at risk.

Another problem has been the cost of living. Census Bureau statistics show that the average household spends more than a third of their income on housing costs, up from about 20% only ten years ago. As a result, financial difficulties such as a job loss, unexpected medical costs, or other emergencies quickly put a homeowner's mortgage in jeopardy. Rising consumer debt burden means any disruption in financial circumstances like unemployment, illness, or divorce can seriously impact a homeowner's ability to make payments -no matter where they live. So look for distressed properties in every neighborhood. They're out there waiting for you to fix and flip!

Secret 17

Just Because a Property is in Foreclosure
<u>Does Not Mean There is Something Wrong With It</u>

As a flipper, you're going to find some of your best deals with houses in foreclosure. But just because a property is in foreclosure does not mean there is something wrong with it. The secret here is that a house's condition has nothing to do with whether it is in foreclosure. Think of it this way. If there is a serious problem with a house (i.e. a major expense such as a roof), and the homeowner can't afford it, why would the homeowner choose foreclosure? The consequences are much too severe. The homeowner could simply sell the property rather than lose it through foreclosure. As you can see, it is a mistake to assume that there is something seriously wrong with a house just because it is in foreclosure.

More likely, there will be minor repairs and cosmetic problems with the properties you will find. The reasons should be obvious. Homeowners in foreclosure don't have the money to properly maintain their properties. So you can expect the house to be in some degree of disrepair (also known as "deferred maintenance"). But in those situations, the repairs are likely minor and won't involve much of an expense. For example, expect to find properties that need the front lawn landscaped, windows replaced, kitchens and bathrooms updated, and floors resurfaced.

Perform your due diligence, follow your instincts, and make an informed evaluation of the flipping potential of each property. If you truly have good reason to believe there's a major problem with a house, move on and focus on purchasing another house. After all, there are plenty of fish in the sea! Don't rely on what the homeowner tells you about the condition of the property, and don't send someone else out to inspect the property for you. You need to see the property with your own eyes, from all four sides, inside and out, in order to have a clear understanding of the property's actual condition. And most importantly, once you have the house under contract, hire a general contractor to inspect the property and give you a professional written opinion before you proceed.

Last, but certainly not least, leave something in your budget to cover the unexpected. That way, you'll always be covered in case you underestimated rehab costs.

Secret 18

Always Inspect the House

You should always thoroughly inspect a house before you purchase it. You should always walk around the exterior of the property first, taking extensive notes as you do. Whenever you perform a walk-around evaluation, make sure to bring a notepad and a camera. Take thorough notes on the:

- General condition of the outside of the house,
- Condition of the paint or siding,
- Condition of the roof, gutters, and downspouts,
- Condition of the windows and doors, and
- Condition of the yard (especially the property's "curb appeal," the first impression it makes from the street)

If you don't have any home repair or construction experience, that's okay. The point of your inspection isn't to spot every possible defect. Your goal at this point is to get a general impression of the condition of the house, noting "deferred maintenance," and to decide whether it's worth flipping. If you decide to purchase it, you will have sufficient time to have a contractor inspect the property and give you his professional opinion before you proceed.

Now take a walk around the exterior of the house. You may not be able to see everything, but if you can, note:

- The appearance of the front yard, side yards, and backyard,
- The presence and condition of the garage,
- The condition of the exterior (paint, siding, roof, windows, doors, etc.),
- The condition of any fences, walls, sheds, or other structures.

Your goal at this initial stage is to assess the property. But it also helps to get a sense of the neighborhood. So take time to look at nearby properties. Are they in good condition? Do the owners appear to be taking care of their homes ("pride of ownership") or are the front yards in various stages of disrepair? Are there a lot of vacant properties or "FOR SALE" signs in the area? Does the neighborhood feel safe? Are there any negative factors, like nearby major highways, manufacturing plants, or excessive traffic?

In some cases, your walk-around inspection will automatically disqualify a house from consideration. If the exterior is in disrepair, it's likely the interior is in poor shape, too. If the exterior is well maintained and cared for, it's likely the interior is in similar condition. In some cases, the house may be unoccupied, and you can look through the windows and doors. If you do peek in the windows, it's a good idea to walk next door and let the neighbors know who you are and what you're doing. Aside from being the courteous and right thing to do, the neighbor may also offer helpful information (and gossip) about the house, the neighborhood, and current market values. It is often amazing (and amusing) what people know about their neighbors!

Once you've thoroughly inspected the exterior, have the homeowner escort you through the interior. The owners are certainly under no obligation to welcome you into their home, but if you approach them with a positive attitude, they will likely invite you inside.

Once inside, bring a clipboard and take extensive notes on each room. Have the homeowner tell you what is good about the room and what needs to be repaired. It is crucial to have the owner tell you what is bad or broken because once negotiations begin, they won't tell you what is wrong with the house. Take extensive notes about everything you see and use your camera or cellphone to take photographs. During the course of your search for flipping candidates, you'll look at a lot of properties. In fact, the more properties you see, the harder it will get to remember the details about each one. As a result, your notes and photos will serve as a valuable reference down the road.

Secret 19

Even If You Can't Get Inside, You Can Still Estimate a Property's Value

If you can't get inside a house (because the homeowner isn't cooperating or some other reason), there are still other methods of estimating a property's value. For example, your real estate agent can help you estimate the fair market value of the house utilizing the *Multiple Listing Service* ("MLS"). The MLS will allow the agent to compare it to similar houses sold and "listed" (i.e. currently for sale) in the neighborhood. This is called the "Sales Comparable" approach to valuation.

The sales comparable approach is based upon analyzing the property's square footage, lot size, bedrooms, bathrooms, and other relevant characteristics in comparison to other houses that recently sold in the neighborhood. Your agent can also assess the property's curb appeal and exterior condition to help make a value estimate. You can then estimate the cost of making common repairs (i.e. replacing carpet, painting walls, and landscaping). To get estimates, call local painters, carpet distributors, and contractors. (Hopefully you already have some of these individuals on your Dream Team.) Explain the project and ask them to estimate the costs.

Some contractors may be reluctant to give you an estimate based on limited information because they'll be concerned you will later try to hold them to that price. If that should occur, explain to them that you're simply trying to assess the opportunity. Assure them that if you purchase the property you will ask them to make a formal estimate. Be sure they understand that you need only a ballpark figure rather than a precise and formal proposal.

In order to determine what you should pay for this house, you need to work backwards. Start with the real estate agent's estimate of market value once the house is rehabbed. This is called the *"After Repaired Value"* (or *"ARV"*). We'll use that figure as the sales price at which you hope to flip the property. Subtract the agent's commission (6%) from the sale price. Then subtract the cost of estimated repairs and rehab, along with the cost of holding the property (i.e. mortgage payments, taxes, insurance, utilities, and so forth). (A mortgage broker can help you determine these estimated costs.) The resulting number is the most you should be willing to pay for the property, if you're willing to break even.

But nobody does this just to breakeven! You are a flipper and expect to make a profit! So, next determine how much you expect to make for your time and efforts. Some flippers want a 20% return, while others expect 30%. The amount of profit you wish to make is a function of your goals, the amount of time you'll need to spend on the project, and, frankly, what a realistic return will be. In other words, be realistic. As a beginner, you should aim for at least 20% return on your initial investments. Later, you can always increase your returns to 30%, 35%, 40%, or more.

If you are unable to inspect the interior, there may be surprises. In this occurs, you should add a contingency amount to the estimated costs for unanticipated expenses. You may decide to add $10,000 to your costs, or 10% of the sales price, or more. Here's a rule of thumb: set aside a $10,000 contingency on each deal. In that way, you're always protected should something unexpected occur.

Let's look at an example to understand how this works in real life. You find a house that meets your criteria for a good flip. A local realtor estimates that the house has a after-repaired value of approximately $300,000 (based upon recent comparable sales and current listings in the neighborhood). You estimate your costs of sale will be approximately $18,000. You estimate that your holding costs will be approximately $3,000 for four months. You also estimate you'll need to spend $10,000 on repairs and upgrades. To be safe, you decide to add $10,000 in contingency costs. Here are your estimated costs:

Market Value: $300,000

Costs:
Repairs: 10,000
Holding: 3,000

Sales: 18,000
Contingencies: 10,000
Profit (20%):   60,000
TOTAL COSTS: $101,000

Purchase price: $199,000

Based on this example, the most you can pay, in order to make a 20% profit ($60,000) on your flip, would be no more than $199,000. If you want to make a 30% profit with this house, you would need to purchase the property for $169,000. If you can purchase the property for less, you lower your risk and potentially increase your profits.

Here's another secret: Always overestimate costs and underestimate profits. This will provide you with an additional cushion, which is especially important for when you are first getting started. Over time, your estimating skills will improve and property values will become second nature to you.

Secret 20

Get An Appraisal Whenever Possible

In theory, a house is worth only what someone is willing to pay for it. Nevertheless, as a flipper, you will want to know more specifically what a property (you're considering purchasing) is really worth. After all, one of the biggest mistakes a new investor can make is not knowing the true market value of a property. There are many different ways of evaluating the after-repaired value of a house. You can do your own research, or ask a realtor for a *"Broker's Price Opinion,"* or better still, you could hire an appraiser for a professional opinion, which is called an *"appraisal."*

Appraisals are an integral part of real estate investing. Lenders use appraisals to make sure they don't loan more than the property is worth. Sellers use appraisals to help them value their properties for sale, and buyers (like you) use appraisals to make sure they don't overpay for a property.

Having a good sense of how appraisals are performed can be helpful to you in estimating value. With this in mind, there are three primary methods appraisers utilize for determining value of a property:

1) Cost Approach,
2) Income Approach, and
3) Sales Comparison Approach.

1. *Cost Approach*. The cost approach determines the value of a property by calculating how much it would cost to replace it. In other words, the cost approach estimates how much it would cost to rebuild the same building on the land. It involves a three-step process.

The first step is to find a piece of land similar to the property you are considering and calculate its value. Because land value cannot be determined by the cost method (land cannot be replaced), the value of the land is determined by using recent sales of comparable land in the area.

The second step involves calculating the cost to rebuild the structure as if it were new. This is typically referenced as a *"cost per square footage"* to build. Keep in mind, the cost to build certain portions of the house are greater (or less) than building other portions of the house. For example, the cost to build the main house will obviously be greater than building the garage.

The third and final step involves deducting an amount for depreciation (i.e. wear and tear) based upon the current condition of the building. The depreciation adjustment is made to reflect that the building being evaluated is not new.

Although the cost approach can be applied to single-family residences, it is most effective for properties that do not have information readily available for the sales approach or the income approach. Cost approach is also useful when a property is fairly unique, such as a church, and suitable comparables in the area can't be found.

2. *Income Approach.* The Income Capitalization Approach estimates the value on a property based on its ability to produce rental income. This approach is commonly used to estimate the value of office buildings, commercial real estate, and multi-unit apartment buildings.

First, the appraiser calculates the gross rental income of the property. Then he subtracts the operating expenses (i.e. mortgage payments, taxes, insurance, utilities, maintenance, insurance, and other costs). The result is the "Net Income" the property will generate per month (or per year):

    Gross income: $300,000
    Expenses: $270,000
    Net income: $30,000 (per year)

Once the appraiser determines the net income, he will then apply a *"Capitalization Rate."* The capitalization rate is the expected rate of return an investor would expect to receive on his investment.

$$\text{Value} = \frac{\text{Net Income}}{\text{Capitalization Rate}}$$

For example, let's say you want to get at least a 10% rate of return on your investments (if you can't, you'd rather invest your money elsewhere). So, if an apartment building generates $30,000 net income per year, and you want a 10% capitalization rate, the value of the property to you would be $300,000 ($30,000 divided by 10%).

$$\text{Value} = \frac{\$30,000}{10\%} = \$300,000$$

In this example, the value of the apartment building to you is $300,000. That's the most you can pay in order to get a 10% rate of return on your investment. In effect, that becomes the value of the property, at least as you wish to utilize it. But what if you're willing to accept a 7% rate of return? Here's the formula:

$$\text{Value} = \frac{\$30,000}{7\%} = \$428,857$$

As you can see, the value of the property would increase to $428,857 ($30,000 income divided by 7% cap rate). In other words, you would be willing to increase your offer to $428,857 in order to achieve a 7% rate of return on your investment.

3. ***Sales Comparison Approach.*** Using the sales comparison approach, the appraiser estimates the value of a property by comparing it to similar properties that recently sold in the area, called *"comparables"* or *"comps."* This approach is the most accurate to determine the value of single-family residences, condominiums and smaller rental buildings (2-4 units).

Appraisers typically compare the subject property to at least three comparable sold houses within a one-mile radius within the past 4-6 months. Since very few houses are identical, the appraiser will adjust the value of the subject property based upon a comparison of various features and amenities. For example, if the subject property has a swimming pool and the comps do not, the appraiser will increase the value of the subject property higher to compensate for the added value of the pool.

Here's a simple example: You're interested in purchasing a three-bedroom, two-bath, 1,500-square-foot home built in 1975 for a quick flip. A similar 1,500-square-foot, three-bedroom, two-bath home built in 1973, located two streets over in the same neighborhood, sold last week for $220,000. In this example, the houses are the same size, have the same number of bedrooms and bathrooms, and are nearly the same age. Roughly speaking, the house you're considering should sell for approximately the same price as the similar house a couple of streets away. As long as the two houses are in similar condition they should be comparable, and their values should be similar. But, if the house you're considering has a two-car garage, and the comps do not, the appraiser may increase the value of your property as much as $1,000 to reflect the added value of the garage.

Keep in mind the appraiser has a reasonable amount of latitude within which to determine the value of the house. Two different appraisers evaluating the same property will rarely arrive at the same exact value.

Here's another secret: Don't try to influence the appraiser. Let the appraiser develop an unbiased appraisal rather than targeting the appraisal to some predetermined value. This practice is illegal, unethical, and harmful to homeowners, neighborhoods, and the local real estate market.

Secret 21

<u>Location, Location, Location</u>

I know you've heard it before, but it bears repeating. The better the location, the more you can improve both the house and its value. If the overall real estate market heats up, better areas appreciate more quickly. When the market cools, better locations tend to hold their value. In less desirable locations, the houses are cheaper and so-called "good deals" are relatively easy to find. But with less desirable areas, you won't be able to get back your investment on anything other than basic improvements (unless you buy significantly below market value).

Many new flippers hope to find a property in need of minor repairs so they can buy cheap and flip for a handsome profit. True, fixing up a house for profit can work if you do your due diligence and handle the repairs wisely. Unfortunately, many new flippers fall into the trap of over-improving a house compared to other houses in the neighborhood. In the end, they have a white elephant on their hands that takes a long time to sell (or requires selling at a loss).

Here are some of the keys to a good location: a) It is close to colleges, upscale shopping, sports, and/or cultural events,

b) Homeowners in these neighborhoods tend to spend significant sums remodeling homes, c) It is close to where young professionals work and want to live, d) Houses stay on the market for a relatively short period of time, and e) Reasonably priced starter homes are hard to find.

One of the largest factors contributing to the desirability of an area is the local school system. An area that has a reputation for good schools will tend to have more homebuyers actively seeking to move there. In fact, when homes are in attractive school districts, Realtors often advertise that fact, knowing they will attract more homebuyers.

A good location with desirable schools tends to create relatively rapid home-appreciation. In a seller's market, these homes will appreciate faster. In a down market, they'll hold their value longer.

In contrast, here are factors that can alert you to less desirable locations: 1) Busy streets and traffic, 2) Houses poorly maintained, 3) Nearby airport, industrial centers, or retail and commercial congestion, 4) Poor school system reputation, 5) Business and industry moving out of the area, 6) Higher-than-average crime rates, and 7) Sellers offering a number of concessions to attract buyers.

With a little investigation (and some input from your real estate agent), you can quickly determine the best neighborhoods in your area. Once you have a feel for it, you don't have to worry that a "good" neighborhood will suddenly become a "bad" neighborhood. Changes take place slowly over time.

Ideally look for "don't-wanter" homes to flip. These are houses the owners want to get rid of so badly that they are willing to accept almost anything. Ideally, you want a don't-wanter home in a "do-wanter" neighborhood. You can often find great deals on properties simply by driving around good neighborhoods, finding don't-wanters, and then talking with the homeowners. Don't-wanters stand out. They often have overgrown front yards, newspapers piled up on the porch, peeling paint, broken windows, and an empty look to them. These are the properties to look for.

In summary, take the time to learn the ins and outs of your area. Location, location, location are still the three most important words in real estate.

Secret 22

Always Do Your Homework Before You Buy

Complacency in flipping houses is dangerous. You watch! The one time you fail to perform your "due diligence," or inspect the interior of a house, or check the chain-of-title, or confirm the sales comparables, or properly calculate the after-repaired value, will be the one time that something goes wrong. In order to avoid potential problems, create a fail-safe system. Create checklists to make sure you have taken all the necessary steps before purchasing a distressed property. Never rest on your laurels and assume you know everything you need to know about a property. This is your money you're investing. Don't look for short cuts.

As the saying goes, knowledge is the experienced investor's best insurance. Experienced flippers double-check value estimates with members of their Dream Team. Experienced flippers take a very close look at the house. Experienced flippers thoroughly inspect the title for such potential problems as mechanics liens, tax liens, junior mortgages, or chain-of-title gaps.

Every transaction is different. Every property is different. Every seller is different. Every deal is different. No matter how long you've been flipping, you'll run across something new. Ask an experienced flipper whether he is ever surprised, and the answer will likely be *"every single day."* In other words, there are no shortcuts to success, especially in flipping properties. Work hard, always do your homework ("due diligence"), and good results will follow.

Secret 23

Always Get Clear Title to the Property

First, let's understand what is meant by *"title"* and *"clear title."* Title is real estate jargon for ownership. It's a fancy way of saying who owns the house. It's like title to your automobile. Title is very important because it establishes the legal owner(s) of the property, along with any liens or claims encumbering that ownership. For example, if you purchased a house using a loan secured by a deed of trust or mortgage, the lender's name appears on the title as a lienholder.

"Clear title" means there aren't any gaps in the chain-of-title or claims against your ownership. *"Chain of title"* refers to previous owners of the property. Before you purchased a property to flip, it probably went through several ownership changes over the years, creating a chain of title. A weak link at any point in that chain could cause problems. Someone along the way may have forged a signature on a deed, or there may be unpaid real estate taxes, or other liens against the property. For example, if Person A sold the property to Person B and then Person C sold the property to Person D, to whom did Person B sell the house? Something's missing, which could indicate a

problem in the chain-of-title. Such a problem could keep you from getting clear title.

Accordingly, you will want to confirm that there are no gaps in the documentation transferring the property between the previous owners. In order to do this, you'll need to examine the documents in the county recorder's office. Better yet, contact a title insurance company and order a Preliminary Title Report ("Prelim").

A prelim is not insurance. It is simply a report from the title company that lays out the title information in an easy-to-read format. Your title company may either charge for the Prelim ($300 to $500) or offer it for free with the understanding that when you buy title insurance, you will buy it from them.

Here's what you should look for when reviewing the Prelim:

1. **Homeowner's names**: Make sure the name on the deed matches the name of the person you are dealing with. If not, you may have a problem.

2. **Date purchased and price paid**: You can get a sense of the property's current value by knowing when it was previously purchased and how much was paid. This will give you a better feel for what the homeowners will hope to get when they sell.

3. ***Deed names***: The names on the deed of trust or mortgage should match the name on the deed. If not, there needs to be a plausible explanation, or you're going to have a problem with title.

4. ***Current first lienholder***: This is the lender holding the senior mortgage on the property. They are senior because their mortgage was recorded in the county recorder's office before any other mortgage. But problems may arise when you're at the foreclosure auction without reviewing the Prelim. For example, what if you're bidding on the foreclosing deed of trust assuming it is the senior lienholder. In actuality, the lender is in a junior position. You may end-up buying the property from this junior lienholder. Not only are you not getting the good deal you thought you were getting, but what if the senior lender is also foreclosing? In that situation, your ownership may be wiped out, leaving you with nothing.

5. ***Second lienholder.*** This is the second (or junior) lender holding a deed of trust or mortgage encumbering the property. They are junior because their deed of trust or mortgage was recorded after the senior lien was recorded (but before any other deeds of trust or mortgages were recorded).

6. ***IRS federal income tax liens***. These are liens recorded by the Internal Revenue Service for unpaid federal income taxes.

7. *State income tax liens*. These are liens recorded by the state for unpaid state income taxes.

8. *Property tax liens*. These are liens recorded by the county for unpaid property taxes.

9. *Other liens*: Mechanics liens (or construction liens) are recorded by contractors and/or suppliers that worked on a property but weren't paid.

Once you've reviewed the Prelim and are comfortable that you will receive clear title if you purchase the property, you will want to purchase title insurance. Title insurance protects against loss arising from problems with title to real estate. It covers the insured party (you) for any claims and legal fees that may arise out of such title problems. Specifically, the insurance protects against losses from events that occurred prior to the date of the policy. In other words, the coverage period ends on the day the policy is issued and extends backward in time for an indefinite period.

In that respect, title insurance works the opposite of life insurance. Life insurance protects against losses resulting from events that occur **after** the policy is issued for a specified time period extending into the future. In contrast, title insurance protects against losses resulting from events that occurred **before** the policy was issued.

For example, what if you hired a contractor to repair the house after you purchased it, but then you did not pay him.

In that event, the contractor could record a mechanic's lien against your house. In that situation, you are not protected by your title policy because the lien was recorded after the date your title insurance policy was issued.

Title insurance also protects against losses that might occur due to another
party claiming ownership of the property. For example, under duress, foreclosing homeowners have been known to defraud investors by selling their property more than once to get extra money. In this scenario, you could end-up purchasing a house from the homeowners after another investor has already bought the property. This would create a legal mess that could be costly to sort out and make it difficult or impossible to get all of your money back. Title insurance helps avoid such nasty and costly surprises.

Title insurance will also pay your legal fees if you have to go to court to defend your title to the property. And if you lose the property, the title insurance will cover your loss up to the amount of your policy.

You may be thinking, 'Wait a minute... *if I pay a title insurance company for a Prelim, why do I need title insurance? Isn't it the company's job to make sure the title is clear?*" Yes, but unexpected problems can pop-up. Title insurance is a cheap way to avoid the cost of major title problems that could occur later. In fact, even if you're purchasing an REO property from a lender, get title insurance so you won't lose out if a lien was not properly recorded against the property, or if something was missed when the Prelim was compiled.

Here another secret; The more you know about a property's title and the more you watch out for potential red flags, the less likely you are to have a problem with title. And always get title insurance to protect yourself from loss.

Secret 24

Distressed Properties Don't Always Need Costly Repairs

If you purchase a house at a foreclosure auction, you're buying it "*as is*" and often without the opportunity to make an inspection. You may have gotten a look at the exterior, but the condition of the interior is completely unknown. You don't know whether the former owners stripped the house of the fixtures, including the toilets and kitchen sink, on their way out the door! Any investor who has flipped more than a few foreclosure properties has experienced at least one horror story.

Now, don't get me wrong, willful destruction does occur, but it is rare. Occasionally, you'll find properties where walls were trashed, appliances removed, toilets and sinks torn-out. Thousands of dollars of work and significant amounts of time required to return the house to marketable condition. This happened because the homeowners resented moving out of their homes involuntarily and expressed that resentment in a destructive way. But in truth, those situations are few and far between.

More commonly, you'll find foreclosure properties in excellent condition after the homeowners vacate. After all, bad things do happen to good people. The homeowners (through no fault of their own) may have lost their house due to illness, a job loss, or some other unexpected occurrence. But financially distressed homeowners are otherwise responsible and caring individuals who treat their homes with respect. They would never consider damaging them when they vacate. Think about yourself for a second. If you lost your home in foreclosure, would you trash it before moving out? I don't think so!

The better approach, if you buy properties at the foreclosure auction, is to be a cautious buyer. Assume you will have to make at least some repairs: replace the carpet, repaint the interior, replace at least a few of the appliances, and make upgrades to the kitchen and bathrooms before you flip.

Experienced flippers also understand they may occasionally need to make major repairs and improvements to a house.

How do you mitigate the risk? One way is to focus on buying directly from homeowners. If you buy directly, you'll have an opportunity to inspect the interior of the house while negotiating with the homeowner. You'll also have an opportunity to inspect the house as they vacate and before you pay them any money.

Here's a secret: another way to protect yourself if you buy directly from a homeowner is to insure the property. The minute you sign a purchase contract with them, purchase property insurance, inventory the contents of the house, and take photos. The insurance will protect the value of the property and its contents. Of course, the insurance agent will drive by to make sure the house isn't obviously damaged already. But, if you have a policy in place and then the homeowner trashes the house on his way out, your policy will help you recover some of your losses. If you expect the worst and factor that into your financial evaluation, you'll come out okay regardless of what a resentful or negligent homeowner may do.

To encourage homeowners to leave the house in good repair when they vacate, offer them some extra cash in exchange for their leaving the house *"broom-clean."* Broom-clean means that the homeowners will not damage or remove anything that is part of the house. They will take all their belongings with them. They will throw away anything they no longer want, and they will sweep and vacuum the house when they vacate. You might even consider hiring a roll-off trash container for their use. Most importantly, don't give them any money until their moving van is in the driveway, their belongings are packed, and they give you the keys. In that way, you can inspect the property, and confirm that they left it broom-clean.

Here's another secret: If you'll really don't want to deal with homeowners, another alternative is to buy an REO property directly from a lender. Lenders get these properties after the foreclosure auction, and hold them in their REO inventory, and then list them for sale with real estate agents. In many circumstances, the lender has made rudimentary repairs to the house, so you can focus on rehab and upgrades.

Secret 25

Watch out for Pre-existing Problems

Every house you consider should be inspected as thoroughly as you can before you consummate the deal. If you can access the inside, thoroughly inspect the interior, room by room. If you can't get inside, you can still inspect the exterior. Get a sense of the neighborhood, assess the quality of schools, and check out local crime rates.

What if you find a property, but the tenants refuse to cooperate. Under these circumstances, you can't set foot on the property, much less inside the house for an interior inspection. But with camera and notebook in hand, you can still evaluate the property from the street:

- The overall impression the property makes ("curb appeal"),
- The condition of the paint, brick, masonry, or siding,
- The roof, gutters, and downspouts,
- The windows and doors,
- The driveway and garage,
- Landscaping, and
- Exterior structures.

During your exterior inspection, check all four sides of the house. Unless the yard is very large or the house is surrounded by a tall fence, you can almost always walk around and see the majority of the house and the lot. Watch out for the following:

Standing water: Standing water around the house is a sign of poor drainage. Poor drainage can cause settling or cracked foundation. Look for damp, mossy areas and areas where grass doesn't grow. Some drainage problems are easy to fix. But if you see standing water, make sure you investigate further.

Water and moisture damage: Rain, snow, and moisture damage can be seen by wood rotting in the soffits (where there's no ventilation), or moss growing on roof shingles or siding. These signs of exterior moisture damage usually indicate problems inside the house, especially in attics. Dampness also promotes the growth of mold and mildew, which creates health risks and is expensive to repair.

Structural problems: During the exterior inspection, look for large cracks in walls, especially in corners. Long horizontal cracks can be a tip-off to foundation movement. Major structural problems, like a cracked or settling foundation, can be very expensive and time-consuming to repair. In fact, unless you can get a firm estimate on repair costs and pay a low price for the house, don't buy the house.

While you're assessing the house, develop an overall impression of its location and the surrounding neighborhood. Try to determine whether the house has potential to sell quickly once you fix it up. For example, if you make cosmetic improvements, will the house appeal to a broader range of buyers? Will prospective buyers feel the neighborhood is attractive and a place they would want to raise their families? Will the house be comparable with other houses in the neighborhood?

Now you can appreciate why it is always beneficial to meet with the homeowners. The meeting will allow you the opportunity to see inside the home! Once you have actual knowledge of the interior condition of the house, you can more realistically negotiate a fair price between you and the homeowner. Even if you don't buy from the homeowner, and ultimately purchase the property at the foreclosure sale, seeing inside will give you an edge over other investors who may be bidding on the property sight unseen.

Secret 26

Treat Your Neighbors Good

When you buy a house and start to make repairs and renovations, don't be surprised if the neighbors stop by. They'll be fascinated not only by the changes you're making to the house (and how it will affect the neighborhood), but also by the fact that you're obviously treating the purchase as an investment. Remember that neighbors would really like to have a say in who lives in the neighborhood. If someone they know (and like) is looking for a home, you can be sure the neighbors will tell them about the home that's currently being fixed-up in their neighborhood.

You'll find that some neighbors will "accidentally" wander by to introduce themselves and see what you're doing. Others will want to check out the rehab taking place, because they would like to make changes to their own homes, and if nothing else, would like to see the ideas, materials, and subcontractors you are using.

So, whatever you do, don't ignore the neighbors! They could potentially refer a buyer to you. But don't talk about what you paid for the house or how much you're spending. Simply say you're *"working hard to make sure the home is safe, clean, well-maintained, and in move-in condition for the next owner."* If a visitor asks what you'll list the property for, a candid answer could be, *"You know, I'm not sure. We've finalized about 90% of our renovation plans, but we are still considering a few options, so I'm not sure yet what a fair price will be. All I'm sure of right now is that we're putting a lot of money and effort into making this home special."*

Conversations like these can often get the neighborhood excited and generate "buzz" even before renovations are complete. Some buyers may want to get in early and purchase the house before you've invested a lot in renovations. In that way, they can pay less for the house, save money by performing renovations themselves, and pick out the carpet, paint, and other materials themselves.

As you can see, your neighbors are your best marketing partners. I've flipped several properties to relatives and friends of neighbors who were referred to me. And don't worry about where you stand in the repair and renovation process when you sell. If you can make a reasonable profit and you're happy with the deal, then sell.

Here's another secret: Work on the exterior first (or start the exterior renovations at the same time you begin renovating the interior). This can generate a great deal of word-of-mouth advertising. If you still haven't sold the home by the time renovations are complete, hold an open house. And be sure to invite all the neighbors!

Section D: Finding Properties

Secret 27

You Don't Need to be an Insider to Find Deals

If a homeowner has defaulted on their mortgage payments, the lender will initiate foreclosure proceedings. These are good properties for you to try to buy and flip. But you don't need to be an insider to find them.

Keep in mind, the foreclosure is public -- these notices must be recorded in the county recorder's office and published in a local newspaper. So this information is readily available to the public for everyone to see. So you don't need to be an insider to get this information. The notices are public and accessible to everyone.

But you can keep your finger on the pulse of your local real estate market and gain *"insider"* knowledge by paying close attention to your market and by building a network of real estate professionals in your area. For example, network with people who commonly assist homeowners in default or in foreclosure, including real estate agents, bankers, bankruptcy attorneys, real estate attorneys, divorce attorneys, other investors, and credit counselors.

Most importantly, become an *insider* by earning a good track record of dealing fairly with distressed homeowners.

Word will spread. Then other homeowners will come to you for assistance, and you won't need to search for them.

Here's another secret: Don't bother driving to the county recorder's office. It is torture dealing with the bureaucracy. Instead, if you want to become a professional flipper, subscribe to a local foreclosure listing service (i.e. Retran.net in Southern California). For a small monthly fee, the listing service will give you internet access to these notices. Plus, they will give you these notices within 1-2 days of recording (as opposed to the newspapers which are often weeks behind).

Secret 28

It is Never Too Early to Find a Good Deal

If you are fortunate to find a distressed property, you'll have time to bring in your Dream Team to help you assess the deal, determine the condition of the house, and arrange financing.

So the earlier the better. The more you know about a house, the better you'll be developing an accurate estimate of how much to pay for it. Plus, by getting involved early in the process, you can immediately begin your due diligence. You'll meet with the homeowners, tour the interior of their house, and determine what repairs will be needed. Further, you will find out what they would like out of the deal, what the lienholders are owed, and calculate your profit when you flip the house. This knowledge will put you in a better position to access the situation and determine the house's ARV ("after repaired value").

You'll undoubtedly find some of your best deals when dealing with homeowners (before the foreclosure auction). If you contact them early enough in the foreclosure process, and offer to purchase the house, not only are you helping the homeowner out of an incredibly stressful situation, but you've also eliminated competition from other flippers.

Sure, there is always the risk that you'll spend time researching a property and working with distressed homeowners only to lose out when the homeowner decides not to sell, or reinstates their loan, or sells to another investor. But this risk is rare. In those circumstances where this does occur, you still had the opportunity to inspect the property thoroughly. As a result, you gained experience determining repair costs, rather than simply estimating. This experience will help you when analyzing other properties in the future.

So don't let this deter you, even if you spent hours analyzing a deal that doesn't go through. You'll have gained valuable experience and developed additional expertise. After all, developing knowledge is never a waste of time.

Secret 29

<u>Foreclosure Notices Are a Great Source for Deals</u>

Some of your best candidates for flipping will come from houses going into foreclosure. You can find out about foreclosure properties by bird-dogging foreclosure notices. As soon as the foreclosure notice is published, it is your official notification that you can contact the homeowner and buy the property. It's like the flashing green light at the beginning of a race. Time to start!

Keep in mind, the foreclosure of most properties in states that use deeds of trust are non-judicial. In other words, the courts are not involved. And because the courts are not involved, there is no service of process or a sheriff serving the homeowner with court papers. Instead, the lender hires a trustee who conducts a non-judicial foreclosure. The trustee is required pursuant to state law to issue a series of notices. These notices are mailed to the homeowner, recorded in the country recorder's office, posted on the property, and published in a local newspaper. These notices are the official announcement to the public that the foreclosure process has begun.

Besides the homeowner, flippers (just like you) also have access to these notices and receive word of the pending foreclosure. In addition, there are web-based services that you can subscribe to that will notify you of foreclosure notices in your area. This is your opportunity to contact the homeowner. In other words, when you see a notice of default or notice of sale, it is your signal to check out the house, contact the homeowner, and start utilizing strategies to purchase that house.

When you spot a foreclosure notice for a house that catches your eye, cut out the notice and add it to a file you create for that house. By monitoring these notices, you can get a better feel for the progression and be ready to buy when the deal is right.

Secret 30

The Best Deals Are Near You

Contrary to popular belief, the best flipping opportunities are right where you live. You don't need to get on planes or trains to find good deals. They are in your own backyard. Think about it. You know the market, the property values, and the right people to help you succeed. Besides, most flippers like to be close to their properties, because it shortens their travel and lets them use their time more efficiently. If you're making repairs to a property you're flipping, wouldn't it be better if it were only 10 - 20 minutes away?

You are most familiar with property values and real estate trends in your area. You'll know what properties are selling for in your area, and you can quickly determine what you're willing to pay for a particular house. And you'll be able to develop a "Dream Team" of local real estate professionals to help you – a team you can call on again and again.

In contrast, purchasing a house in another city or county may require you to find a different contractor, realtor, title company, mortgage broker, attorney, etc. Why waste time putting a new team together?

Every day, properties become available all over the place! While there may be great opportunities in other areas, there are great opportunities in your area, too. And no one has a better feel for which neighborhoods have flipping potential than you. You'll know whether:

- New homes are under construction.
- Owners are adding to the value of their homes by making repairs, additions, and landscaping improvements.
- Yards are well-kept and street are clean and litter free.
- Shopping, parks, and commutes are convenient.
- Crime rates are low and the area is relatively safe.
- The schools have a good reputation.
- New industries are moving in, bringing new growth and opportunities.

Keep in mind, real estate trends constantly change. And nobody knows the local trends better than you! You could decide to buy a distressed property in a lower to middle-class area of town because you know real estate values are on the rise. By knowing your area, you'll see, recognize, and profit from those trends. You also know which areas to avoid.

Most importantly, investing in your own neighborhood can be very rewarding. Neighborhoods with lots of vacant properties can transform into crime-ridden slums almost overnight. By buying, fixing up, and flipping houses, you ensure that abandoned homes do not fall into disrepair, you encourage new families to move in, and you keep the riff-raff out. Plus, as your neighbors see the good you doing, they will be more open to approaching you in the event that they (or someone they know) need to sell their homes.

Secret 31

Buy the Property Directly from the Homeowner Prior to the Foreclosure Auction

One great flipping technique is to buy properties from homeowners before the foreclosure auctions. The time period between the notice of default/sale and the foreclosure auction is known as the *foreclosure pending stage.* The length of this stage is different in every state. During this period, purchases of foreclosure properties are in many ways similar to a normal real estate purchase. You negotiate directly with the homeowner, sign a purchase contract, and proceed with the transaction. The main difference is that instead of the homeowner deciding voluntarily to sell the property, the homeowner is forced to sell because he's confronting losing his home in foreclosure.

You can easily find homeowners in the early stages of foreclosure by checking foreclosure notices in the county recorder's office. The foreclosure notice will list the borrower's name and address, and you can contact them directly. You can also contact the trustee for additional information about the property, but don't be surprised if she's not particularly friendly or cooperative. The trustee provides foreclosures services to the lender, not flippers like you. The trustee is paid to prepare the notices and conduct the trustee's sale, not to act as a real estate information hotline.

So if you're interested in a foreclosure property, the best strategy is to contact the homeowner directly. But keep in mind, the homeowner is under severe pressure and is not likely, at least at first, to respond positively to your approach. You'll need to be tactful, respectful, and aware at all times that the homeowner is under a great deal of stress and strain. Visualize a deer caught in the headlights of an on-coming car and you'll get the picture. So please, be sensitive to their predicament.

Why the stress? Because most homeowners don't want to lose their homes. They will desperately hold onto the hope that things will somehow work out. They are also embarrassed they're facing foreclosure, even if they find themselves in that position through no fault of their own. They are under severe financial pressure and confronting the very real possibility that they will lose their home if they don't do something fast.

If the homeowner is receptive to your approach, the first thing you'll need to determine is the current market value of the property. Next, you will need to deduct all of the existing liens to determine whether the homeowner has any equity remaining in the property. Let's say, for example, that the home has a fair market value of $200,000. You've been able to inspect the home, and other than cosmetic repairs, it's in good shape. You estimate you'll spend $20,000 getting the house ready to flip. You decide you want to make at least 20% profit. So, you decide your walk-away price is $140,000, which leaves you room to make the profit you want while covering repair and holding costs. In this scenario, you offer the homeowner cash for his equity subject to the existing liens.

But if the homeowner still owes $220,000 on the mortgage, you're not likely to buy it for $140,000. In this scenario, the homeowner is underwater. In other words, his home is worth less than the balance of the loan. Here, you'll need to approach the lender to accept a *"short sale."* A what? A short sale is a sale of the property at its current market value. The lender waives the amount their loan exceeds your purchase price. Why would a lender accept a short sale and lose money? Simple, the cost to foreclose would be greater than the proceeds they would receive from the short sale. In fact most lenders prefer a short sale rather than losing more money through a foreclosure sale.

As you can see, buying while the foreclosure is pending does have several advantages. The homeowner may be desperate and willing to accept less than the full amount of their equity. In addition, you can enter the property to inspect it before purchasing (unlike when you buy at the foreclosure sale). And, if you contact the homeowner directly before the homeowner has listed the property with a realtor, the homeowner avoids paying commissions, which could allow you to purchase the property for a lower price. (The average realtor commission is 6% which would come to $12,000 on a $200,000 sales price.)

Buying foreclosure properties can be a win-win-win situation for you, the homeowner and the bank. You may be able to find great deals, the homeowner can escape a foreclosure, and the lender avoids another REO.

But before you contact the homeowner, keep these things in mind:

+ *Treat the homeowner with respect and dignity.* Don't take advantage of these people during this incredibly vulnerable period in their lives. Always remember the adage *"what goes around, comes around."* Use the Golden Rule; treat homeowners as you would like to be treated, and you can't go wrong.

+ *Never mislead the homeowners.* Never represent yourself as a lawyer, realtor, appraiser, or financial advisor (unless, of course you are). State up front that you're an investor and plan to sell the house after you rehab it.

+ *Don't make friends with the homeowner.* Never make friends with them solely to convince them to sell the property to you.

+ *Always recommend that the homeowner contact his attorney to get advice.* Don't try to circumvent other interested parties.

+ *Put all agreements and offers in writing.* In real estate transaction, verbal agreements are *"worth the paper they're written on."*

Let the homeowner decide what is best for them. Don't simply look out for your best interests. Your goal is a win-win result. Always discuss other options they have, but don't try to influence their decision. In this and in all matters, represent yourself professionally and with integrity.

Secret 32

There is Always Enough Time to Buy a Foreclosure Property

It is NEVER too late! Distressed homeowners and lenders are begging for flippers (just like you) to step forward and purchase these properties before they are sold at auction. After all, no one wins if the property is foreclosed. The homeowner loses their home and ruins their credit, while the lender takes back another REO they'll be forced to sell at a loss.

You also need to anticipate that many homeowners will call you at the last minute. It is the nature of our business. Homeowners procrastinate and procrastinate until just days before the foreclosure sale, then realize it's too late to do anything, and call you in desperation. So while other inexperienced investors refuse to get involved because there isn't enough time, you should see it as an excellent opportunity! In fact, you should become a specialist in last minute deals. In other words, although it may be too late for the homeowners, it is never too late for you.

Besides, "too *late*" is really just a function of how much time you need to thoroughly analyze the deal. If you don't have time to estimate value, estimate repair costs, and line up financing, then, yes, it is too late. Time to move on to the next deal. But if you can put together estimates that you're comfortable with, perform your due diligence, and have your financing in place, then it's never too late to capitalize on a great opportunity. If needed, you can contact the lender directly, and request that the foreclosure auction be postponed for 30 days so that you can complete the transaction. Most lenders will be grateful to receive that call and temporarily postponed the foreclosure sale.

It's also smart to keep emotions out of your decision. Rather speed is of the essence, especially in areas where you face competition from other flippers. How do you act quickly and yet make rational and unemotional decisions? Experience is a critical factor. But so is developing a process for evaluating opportunities. The more familiar you are with your area, the quicker you'll be able to estimate property values. Experienced flippers who keep up with local trends and market conditions can often estimate a property's value (without seeing the interior) within 5% - 10%. If you're inexperienced, you should work with a realtor, who can help you estimate a property's value.

As your experience grows, you'll learn how to estimate repairs and renovations to the house. But for now, you can simply estimate $7 per square foot when estimating repair costs for properties you don't have time to inspect. For example, assume that a 1,500-sqnare-foot house will need $10,500 (1,500 x $7) in repairs to get it ready for flipping.

The next time a desperate homeowner calls you the day

before the foreclosure auction and agrees to sell their home, don't turn him down! Tell him you're ready to buy and schedule an appointment immediately!

Secret 33

Think Outside the Box

Every deal is different. But not every deal is a good deal! In some cases, no matter how hard you look at a house, you won't see an opportunity for profit when you flip. If that's the case, walk away and look for a better deal. Always remember to evaluate, estimate, and ask others for advice. In the end, don't enter into any deal unless you're confident you can make a profit when you flip the house. But at the same time, don't walk away too quickly. Do your homework and think *"outside the box."* In other words, take the extra time to look deeper for what other investors may have missed. You may be pleasantly surprised!

A few years ago, I was evaluating a possible deal. The property in question was a single-family residence in Downey, California. The house was in decent shape and had a huge backyard. But it had five bedrooms and five bathrooms. The house had an after-repaired value of approximately $250,000, while other houses in the neighborhood were worth less than $300,000. The mortgage payment was $2,000 per month. On the surface, it didn't look like a good deal. It was the proverbial *"white elephant"*!

Time to think outside the box. First, I researched comparable rentals in the neighborhood by studying the classified section of the newspaper and talking to local realtors. I learned that a 3-bed/2-bath house would rent for $1,500 per month. A 4-bed/3-bath house would rent for $1,600 per month. But there weren't any five bedroom houses in the neighborhood. And even if there were, it is unlikely they would rent for much more than $1,700 per month. After all, there are very few families that need a 5-bedroom house.

Yikes, how could I ever make any money flipping this property? How could this house be a good deal? I started having serious doubts. Nevertheless, the house was there and the owner was eager to sell.

I was just about to say "no," and walk away, when ironically I spotted an advertisement in the newspaper that jumped out at me. It was an ad for a "sober-living" facility. The ad was offering rooms in a house for $500 per month. A light bulb went off in my head! If I could convert this house into a sober-living facility, it would increase its value enormously.

I contacted the facility advertised in the newspaper, and they referred me to the county social services department. I then contacted social services and they gave me their requirements to qualify (which were surprisingly simple and straight forward). I decided to purchase the house after all. I went back to the homeowner and completed an equity purchase of the property. I then rehabbed the property.

Several months later I flipped it to a young entrepreneur looking to expand his sober-living facilities.

As you can see, a property that initially looked like a white elephant turned out to be a very good deal once I was willing to think *"outside the box."* The secret here is to always keep your mind open to opportunities when you find a property for sale. What might appear on the surface to be a bad deal may be a very profitable opportunity once you do your research and think creatively.

Section E: Realtors

Secret 34

You Don't Need Realtors to Find Properties

If you're looking for foreclosure properties to flip, you don't need real estate agents. Think about it this way. There are four stages in the foreclosure process in which to purchase properties. Let's analyze each stage separately and determine whether a realtor is really needed. You may be surprised with the result:

1. ***Stage 1 (Default Stage).*** At the Default Stage, the homeowner has missed his mortgage payments, but foreclosure proceedings haven't started as yet. In most cases, these people haven't contacted a realtor or listed their house for sale. So a realtor won't be very helpful. Besides, if a realtor has already listed the house for sale, you may not want it anyway because it is probably listed at market value. (Remember, we only buy "wholesale," not retail, so that we can make really good deals.) Realtors can't help you find properties that you want to buy wholesale. You need to do that on your own.

2. ***Stage 2 (Foreclosure).*** During this stage, the house is already in foreclosure and a foreclosure sale is pending. The foreclosures notices are recorded in the county recorder's office, published in local

newspapers, and available through foreclosure listing services. So you can find these properties on your own. You don't need realtors.

3. ***Stage 3 (Foreclosure Auction)***. The foreclosure sale is the actual auction of the property on the courthouse steps. The date, time and location of the sale are recorded in the recorder's office, published in a local newspaper, and available through foreclosure listing services. So you don't need a realtor to alert you to properties to be sold at foreclosure auction. You can get this information on your own. Likewise, the auction is open to the public, so obviously you don't need a realtor to help you bid.

4. ***Stage 4 (REO)***. Once a house is sold to the foreclosing lender it is called an "REO" which stands for *"real estate owned"* by the lender. The trick here is to negotiate directly with the asset manager in the lender's REO Department and to do it <u>before</u> they list the property with a realtor. That's where you'll find the real deals! (Once the REO property is listed with a realtor, it is typically marked back up to retail, and we never buy retail!) So avoid realtors who are selling REOs (unless they show a property listed substantially below market).

As you can see, you really don't need realtors to acquire foreclosure properties. But don't get me wrong, you still need realtors. They are invaluable, just not in the way you may think.

Real estate agents will accomplish three important tasks for you: 1) they will advise you of short sales. Those are properties that are worth less than the balance of the loan. Because realtors have access to the Multiple Listing Service, they know about short sale properties before anyone else. And best of all, because the lenders end-up paying their commissions, the realtors work for you for free. So call every realtor you know right now and ask them to find you short sales. 2) Realtors can help you flip properties once you've rehabbed them. Nobody markets and sells properties at retail like realtors. This is their specialty, so why not take advantage of it. You will pay them a commission, but it's worth it, particularly if you're in a hurry to flip a property and need to receive market value. 3) Realtors are really good in giving you sales comparables for properties you're interested in acquiring. Not only do they know what comps recently sold, but also what properties are currently listed. Nobody does it faster and more efficiently than a realtor.

As you can see, Realtors are invaluable to you as a flipper. Likewise, you are valuable to realtors because you are a source of repeat business and tend not to get emotional in your selling decisions. So make a realtor a member of your "Dream Team."

Secret 35

Realtors Don't Have the Best Deals

Contrary to popular belief, real estate agents don't always have the inside track. In fact, in some ways, agents are at a major disadvantage. For example, properties in foreclosures are public knowledge. You have ready access to all the information available if you know where to look.

Consider this: If you're a part-time flipper, all you have to do is focus on finding good deals in your spare time. In contrast, a successful agent is too busy to flip properties. They have to focus on finding homeowners that want to sell, listing properties, marketing, working with potential buyers, and getting escrows closed on time. They don't have time to search out properties to flip and purchase them.

Say you're interested in a new home. You contact an agent and ask to be shown properties that meet your price range, your family's needs, with the amenities you want, and so on. First the agent must find suitable properties for you to view. Then, since you probably work during the day, you are only available to view properties at night or on the weekends. And you're not the only client the agent has. So in all likelihood, the agent spends most days working with clients, getting escrows closed, talking to lenders, most evenings and weekends showing properties, preparing offers, and handling the incredible amount of paperwork and clerical tasks to support these activities. And since you want your new home to be perfect, you may need to look at 10 to 20 homes before you can make a decision. Worse, some of those homes you may look at two, three, or even four times. As you can see, good agents are very busy working with existing clients. Plus, they must always focus on finding new clients, since without new clients the agent's business (and income) will dry up.

There are a lot of great deals out there! Don't let the thought of real estate agents beating you to an opportunity be a deterrent. While it is true that you may occasionally compete with a real estate agent for a deal, it's much more likely you'll be competing with other flippers ad real estate investors like yourself.

Once you've done this long enough, you'll appreciate that the market holds far more opportunities than you have the time, energy, and resources to pursue.

Secret 36

You Don't Need Realtors to Buy Foreclosure Properties

Although foreclosure properties make great flipping candidates, you don't need real estate agents to buy foreclosures. Most realtors don't bother with foreclosure properties because there simply isn't enough time. Realtors typically need 4-6 months to successfully sell a property, yet foreclosure occurs in less than four months. Because of this shortened time period, homeowners attempt to sell their homes on their own (*"For Sale By Owner"* or *"FSBO"*) and typically with disastrous results. Occasionally, you will find a foreclosure listed with a realtor. But avoid those properties because you probably won't be able to purchase them substantially below market.

If the homeowner is unable to sell the home before the foreclosure auction, she loses the right to sell her home because at the auction ownership transfers to the highest bidder. Or, if no one bids, ownership transfers to the lender. If the lender takes ownership, the property becomes a real-estate-owned ("REO") property. At that point, the lender will likely list the property with an agent.

So the most common time realtors get involved is if the bank hires them to list an REO property that it acquired at a foreclosure auction. But again, you don't need to work with realtors. In fact, avoid realtors that have REOs if those properties are already marked-up to retail. Of course, there are always exceptions to a rule. So if you find an REO listed with a realtor that is listed below market, that house would be a good candidate for flipping.

Your other choice is to learn how to contact asset managers at lenders' offices and buy REO properties <u>before</u> they list their properties with a realtor. In fact, some flippers do quite well buying REO properties directly from lenders.

As you can see, you don't need to contact realtors to find foreclosure properties. You can do it on your own and probably with more success! To find foreclosure properties for sale, check your local newspapers, or search for foreclosure notices at your county recorder's office, or better still, sign-up for a foreclosure listing service. In that way, you'll have more foreclosures properties than you'll know what to do with!

Secret 37

You Can Find Good Deals Through Realtors

Actually, you can make good deals by using realtors, but you must pick and choose carefully. Consider this: distressed homeowners have limited options if they want preserve their credit and any equity they have in their homes. They recognize that their options are limited. Their most realistic option is to sell the house, and sell it as quickly as possible! In order to accomplish this, homeowners will either list their properties with realtors to sell, or attempt to sell themselves (*"For Sale By Owner"* or *"FSBO"*). So if you are in a position to close quickly, and have the financing, you have a distinct advantage over other interested parties and can make a good deal.

You also have the opportunity to buy at below market value. Let's say the average home in your area stays on the market for four months. Let's also assume that the homeowner needs to sell their home in less than two months. One factor of how long a home takes to sell is price. As a rule of thumb, houses priced below market value sell more quickly, houses priced at market value sell close to the area's average time on market, and those priced above market value will remain unsold forever. So in order to sell this home quickly, the agent will likely recommend pricing the home below market value. (How far below is a function of how quickly the homeowner needs to sell.)

So if you want a good deal, you need to move quickly. As you now know, properties priced below market sell quickly. So you'll need to be able to act fast. Lining-up financing ahead of time is critical. Spend time with your mortgage broker and ask what you can do to put yourself in a position to purchase a house as quickly as possible. Then take the steps that she recommends. At the very least, you should be *"preapproved"* for a loan amount that will cover the purchase price. And make sure she gives you the pre-approval in writing so that can include it with your offer.

The next step is to make offers, lots of them. Remember, you won't catch any fish if you don't put your hook in the water. And don't be afraid to make offers that are significantly lower than the listing price. Now I don't mean crazy offers that are 50% or more below the asking price. I'm talking about offers that are 20 to 30% below the listing price. You may find your offer is accepted, particularly with a distressed homeowner that needs to sell quickly. As long as you can close quickly, the deal can be yours. Worse comes to worse, you can always negotiate an extension with the lender to allow your transaction to close.

Realtors are also helpful in another common situation. For example, suppose your lowball offer would require the owner to sell at a loss. In that situation, the real estate agent may be able to negotiate a short sale with the lender.

Lenders will agree to a short sale if they can get the bad loan off their books and avoid another costly REO.

Section F: Deals

Secret 38

Regardless Whether Real Estate is Increasing or Decreasing,
There are Always Good Deals

From a flipping point of view, you shouldn't care whether real estate markets are increasing or decreasing. Your only concern should be whether a potential deal makes good financial sense. In other words, with the right strategy, you can make profitable flips regardless of whether the real estate market is going up or going down.

So, let's say values have fallen sharply and there is a glut of homes on the market in your area. Should you buy a property? Well, no matter where you live, what the economic conditions are, and what the real estate market is like, the answer is always the same: ***It depends.***

In other words, no matter which direction the market is trending, always do your homework. It's called "due diligence." For example, if you plan on flipping a house, realistically assess the property's value, the cost of holding and keeping up the property, your eventual sales price, and then determine whether the deal makes good financial sense. Of course, no deal is a sure winner or loser. The answer to the question "*Is this a good deal?*" should always be "*It depends,*" at least until after you've done your homework!

On the other hand, you are not required to flip. Your strategy may be to hold the house and rent it out. With this strategy, your concern should be whether you can obtain sufficient rental income so that the property has a positive cash flow each month. When you're doing your homework, explore what's happening with rental properties in your area. People always need a place to live, and more people rent than own. So as long as the area is not seeing a mass exodus, there are probably a majority of residents looking to rent rather than to buy. In that case, instead of "flipping" the house, consider shifting to a "buy-and-hold" strategy and leasing the property (at least until the market turns around and then you can flip). Keep in mind, as demand for rental properties increases, so do rents.

Say you live in an area where values are falling and every real estate agent in town says it's a buyer's market (i.e. the supply of homes is much greater than the demand). But then a friend refers you to a distressed homeowner who is willing to sell his home $60,000 below its current market value. You determine that the house needs only minor rehab and that you could flip it quickly below market and make a good profit. Should you buy it?

Based on the information presented here, the answer is yes,

even though the real estate market is stagnant and values are decreasing. The risk is relatively low, the return is relatively high, and you feel good about the possibilities for a quick flip based on your pricing strategy.

As you can see above, you shouldn't make a decision on any flip without analyzing the risks, rewards, and potential profit involved. Remember, you're not doing this for fun; you're doing it to get a return on your time and investment! The lesson here is to always put a pen to paper and do your due diligence. If you do that, you won't go wrong.

Secret 39

Structure Your Deals to Make a Reasonable Profit

You can make great deals flipping properties. You buy a house for significantly less than its market value, rehab it to increase its market value, and then flip it for a profit. Yes, you can make fabulous profits, but your profits aren't assured just because you purchased the house at a low price. A flip is like any other investment. The formula is simple and straight forward:

Selling Price - Costs = Profit

A profit is not assured until the purchase price is in your hand, and the purchase price is greater than all your costs. So don't let your expectations get out of hand. Be realistic. Always overestimate expenses and underestimate profits so you are not disappointed by the outcome. Being pleasantly surprised beats being disappointed.

As a flipper, you make a profit only if you sell the property for more than all your costs (i.e. the purchase price, loan payments, fees, taxes, insurance, repairs, renovations, real estate commissions, and the value of your time). In contrast, if you spent more than you sold it for, you lose money. It's that simple.

If you purchased at the foreclosure auction, the risk is you probably didn't inspect the interior of the house prior to the auction. Properties bought at the foreclosure auction are purchased "*as is*," and if major problems exist, those problems become yours. The homeowners could have failed to maintain the property or purposely damaged it when they vacated. Major environmental problems could also exist. For example, there could mold in the walls which could cost thousands of dollars to remove and environmentally remediate.

Even if you purchased directly from the homeowner, and inspected the property thoroughly, you could still encounter risks. For example, while you're renovating the property, changes in the real estate market could cause home prices to fall. In a matter of months, the home you felt sure you could sell for $200,000 may have a market value of $190,000 or less. If you estimated you would make $10,000 in profit that profit has evaporated. To protect yourself and ensure you've created a buffer against unforeseen expenses, always factor in the following costs:

+ Repair and renovation expenses.

+ Holding costs: property taxes, loan interest, insurance, utilities, and so on. Calculate the holding costs for the entire time it will take to make repairs and renovations (2-4 months), and the time you and your agent estimate it will take to sell the property (1-2 months).

\+ Real estate commissions (when you sell).

\+ Transfer taxes.

\+ Fees for title insurance and any other documents.

\+ Recording fees.

\+ Miscellaneous expenses.

\+ Profit. While profit isn't an expense, you should factor in an amount for what you hope to make. If you're new to flipping, plan to make at least 20% on every deal (more as you become more experienced).

Secret 40

Besides the Purchase Price, There Are Other Costs You Must Consider

When flipping properties, you also need to consider repair costs, holding costs, real estate commissions, closing costs, estimated profit, and lost opportunity costs. Let's analyze each of these costs separately.

Repair costs. The rehab costs will likely be your largest cost, so you need to calculate them carefully. If you're able to inspect the interior, you'll be able to estimate the repairs and renovations needed to make the house salable. However, if you aren't able to inspect the interior, use 10% of the purchase price as your estimate of repair costs. In the alternative, multiply the square footage of the house by $7.00. For example, if the property has 1,500 square feet, the estimated repair cost would be $10,500.

Holding costs. It's going to take you approximately 2-4 months to repair, market, and sell the property. During those months, you'll incur holding costs (i.e. mortgage payments, taxes, insurance, and utilities). Neophyte flippers frequently forget to include these costs in their budgets. If you're worried about these costs, you can significantly reduce them by living in the house during this period, which is exactly what many flippers do when they are just starting out. Instead of chalking up your monthly expenses as holding costs, simply consider it rent. Another way to trim your holding costs is to price the house correctly the first time. By offering the best home in its class at the best price, you'll sell the home faster and lower your holding costs to more than cover the cost of selling the home for a little less.

Real estate commissions. You can assume you'll pay a 6% commission to your real estate agent for selling the house when you flip it. For that money, the agent will market your property for sale, list it in the Multiple Listing Service and related websites, advertise in local newspapers, receive and submit offers, negotiate with the buyer, and assist you with the timely close of escrow.

Closing costs. You will incur closing costs when it comes time to sell the property. These costs include escrow fees, title insurance, transfer tax, recording fees, and other miscellaneous charges. For a rough estimate of closing costs, figure 2% of the anticipated selling price.

Estimated profit: While we're at it, let's factor in profit. You want to make at least a 20-25% profit on each of your flips. In that way, if unexpected expenses do pop-up, you'll have some margin before you lose money on the deal. (And if you sell the house for more than you expected, or your expenses are lower, you'll make an even better profit.)

Lost opportunity costs: Opportunity cost is the cost of pursuing one investment choice instead of another. Every investment you make has an opportunity cost. With respect to flipping, lost opportunity cost boils down to making choices between various deals. For example, if you are considering two potential deals and can only make one, which one is likely to generate the greatest return? Which deal fits best into your workload, your skill set, and the time you have available? If you can spend the same amount of time and money on a house that will generate a 20% return instead of another house that will yield only a 10% return, which would you choose?

Time: Another cost that you may not have considered is your time. Successful flipping takes time. If you buy a house and plan to do some repairs yourself, you will save money on repair costs but you'll also spending your time. How much is your time worth? If you'll spend 300 hours repairing and renovating a house and will make $3,000 in profit, your time was worth $10 per hour. If that sounds good to you, great! If it doesn't, you'll need to adjust your cost estimates accordingly. For example, if your time is worth $50 per hour, you should factor $15,000 into your budget for those same 300 hours.

Secret 41

You Can Find Good Deals in the Bankruptcy Court

Although not recommended for the beginner flipper, you can find potential properties to flip in the Bankruptcy Court. But, before you get started, you must know what you're doing.

First, you need to understand that homeowners file bankruptcy because it automatically stops collection actions, most commonly a pending foreclosure. At that point, all of the real and personal property becomes part of the debtor's bankruptcy estate, subject to claims of creditors.

But if you think about it, the debtor's creditors don't want the property. They want their money back! So a bankruptcy trustee is appointed by the court to handle the sale of the debtor's non-exempt assets. The trustee's goal is to maximize the money in the debtor's estate to satisfy as many creditors as possible in the shortest period of time. In order to do that, the property is often sold to satisfy creditors. So the bankruptcy trustee will attempt to sell the debtor's real property as quickly as possible. As a result, there are some great deals to be found in bankruptcy cases, if you know where to look.

The only caveat is that the property be sold for a fair price and subject to bankruptcy court approval. Court approval means that the creditors (and their attorneys) can object to the sales price and/or terms. So, if you make an offer it needs to be fair and reasonable. The only other potential problem is that other investors may come into court at the 11th hour and submit competing bids. So buyer beware.

To navigate the bankruptcy waters, you'll need to work hard to get the trustees, the attorneys, and sometimes even the homeowners, to look favorably upon you and your offer. In addition, you'll need to make sure everything you do is reviewed and approved by a skilled attorney who specializes in bankruptcy law.

As you can see, investing in bankruptcy properties is not for beginners. Instead of dealing with distressed homeowners, you'll be dealing with attorneys and court-appointed trustees, all of whom are committed to getting the highest price possible for the property. What seems simple can become a tangled and complicated web. So, if you're new to flipping, wait until you have some experience under your belt and an attorney who specializes in bankruptcy in your corner.

With that said, you can find great flipping opportunities in the bankruptcy courts, if for no other reason than most investors steer clear due to the effort involved. If you're going to purchase properties in bankruptcy, start networking with bankruptcy attorneys.

Secret 42

Bankruptcy Properties Are Good Deals

Homeowners in bankruptcy are essentially buying time to restructure their finances and relieve the pressure from bill collectors and other creditors. At the same time, their assets are frozen. The non-exempt assets are now considered to be part of the *"Debtor's Estate"* and must be sold to pay off outstanding creditors. But the property cannot be sold without bankruptcy court approval. If you were negotiating with the owner to buy the home prior to the bankruptcy filing, those negotiations are now dead. That opportunity is now lost. From here on you'll be dealing with the bankruptcy court and/or the trustee for the estate.

Once bankruptcy is declared, in essence the owners turn the house over to a court-appointed trustee. The trustee is an attorney in charge of either liquidating the assets to pay off debts (Chapter 7) or restructuring the debt to formulate a reasonable payment plan (Chapter 13). In some cases, homeowners can save their home in bankruptcy. Most of the time however, the home is sold at a bankruptcy auction or at a formal hearing. So, like any other investment opportunity, whether you get a good deal depends on the value of the house and the price you can buy it for.

Two main types of bankruptcy are available to homeowners. Let's take a quick look at each type:

1. ***Chapter 7 Bankruptcy***: Homeowners filing Chapter 7 turnover control of all their non-exempt assets to a court-appointed trustee. The trustee's role is to liquidate assets to pay off creditors' claims against the debtor's estate (the homeowner). Claims can include unpaid mortgages, credit card debt, back taxes, and any other financial obligations.

Control of the property is transferred to the trustee for liquidation. The trustee must make a decision with respect to the debtor's real property. If there is equity, the trustee will sell the house and use the sale proceeds to pay off creditors. If there is no equity, the trustee will abandon the house and allow the lender to proceed with their foreclosure. If the trustee decides to sell, he will usually select the best offer for the property that is most likely to close the fastest. If you want to purchase the house, your offer must be approved by the trustee and court. At this stage, creditors can object to your sales price, but the judge can overrule those objections if he sees fit.

Your best opportunity for getting a good deal is at the liquidation stage, since the homeowners are no longer involved. The trustee is simply interested in selecting the best offer, and the creditors are motivated to get as much of their money back as possible.

If another investor purchases the house, your chances of buying it are effectively over. But a creditor may buy or be given the property, and you may be able to purchase it from that creditor. While you may have to pay more than the creditor paid, the premium may be small because many creditors would prefer to take a relatively low price to avoid the time, cost, and hassles of selling the house on their own.

2. *Chapter 13 Bankruptcy*. Unlike Chapter 7 debtors, homeowners filing Chapter 13 wish to restructure their debts and retain their assets. Under the supervision of the Court, homeowners make arrangements with their creditors to repay their obligations, typically within 36 months (called a "Chapter 13 Plan"). Nevertheless, during the process of re-structuring their debts, they may come to the conclusion that they need to sell their home.

Once the bankruptcy petition has been filed, the homeowners remain in possession and can accept offers and negotiate to sell their house. If you want to purchase their home, you'll work directly with the homeowner (and their attorney). Once you have a deal with the homeowner, it will need to be submitted to the Bankruptcy Court for approval. The attorney, or Chapter 13 trustee, must notify creditors and the creditors must approve the sale (since they now have a vested interest in the proceeds). However, because the creditors are involved, the odds are relatively slim that all parties will approve an offer that's substantially below market value.

As you can see, buying bankruptcy properties takes experience and a good bankruptcy lawyer in your corner. But great opportunities do exist. So once you gain experience you could find that you enjoy the complexity, and profits, to be found in buying properties through the bankruptcy court.

Secret 43

<u>Not Every Property Is a Good Deal</u>

Perhaps the biggest misconception is that just because a house is for sale is a good deal. That's naive. The fact is that you need to do your research ("due diligence") to determine if a property is a good deal. Just like with any other house, you need to know exactly what you're buying, how much it will cost to rehab, how much you can flip it for ("after-repaired value"), and how much of a profit you can reasonably expect. Novice flippers usually get burned when they fail to properly analyze these factors.

In reality, flipping is no different from any other type of investing. You need to carefully calculate your profits. With flipping, your profit comes from the difference between the purchase price and the sale price. That difference must be large enough to cover all your costs and still generate sufficient profit for you. It's that simple.

Some available properties are terrible deals because you'll never recover your costs and make a profit. Others properties are great deals because you can buy significantly below market value, make needed improvements, and then flip for a reasonable profit. The only way to determine the possibilities is to analyze each opportunity. Here's the formula:

Sale Price - Purchase Price + Costs = Profit

Each of the three variables (Sale Price, Purchase Price, and Costs) is made up of smaller components. Some, like the purchase price, you have direct control over because you will determine what you're willing to pay. The price you'll eventually sell the house for (Sale Price), on the other hand, must be estimated. You can check out sales comparables in the surrounding neighborhood to predict the ARV (the "after-repaired value") of the house. But in the end, the true value of a house is what a buyer is *"ready, willing, and able"* to pay when you're ready to sell.

As a flipper, you must purchase the house at a low enough price to afford the holding costs and the necessary rehab and still make a profit. If you plan to upgrade the house, you must have a low enough purchase price so it supports the planned improvements, and still leaves room for profit. On the other hand, if you have no chance of making a profit, you shouldn't purchase the house (regardless of the deal).

Costs are the next variable in the profit equation, which include holding the house, making repairs and improvements, insurance and taxes, mortgage payments, and costs of sale. Some costs are easier to calculate than others. Let's briefly analyze these costs:

Holding Costs: Holding costs include mortgage payments, taxes, insurance, and utilities. How long you hold the house determines the extent of the total cost. Many investors assume they'll hold a house for at least four months, assuming two months to make repairs and two months to flip the house. Your real estate agent and contractor can help you estimate the time it should take to make repairs and flip the property. Keep in mind, how quickly a property sells is often a function of price. If you list the house at below fair market value, you'll sell more quickly. In contrast, if you list the property above market value, you'll hold the property for a longer period of time.

Repairs and Improvements: Cosmetic improvements are relatively inexpensive and can be completed within weeks, if not days. In contrast, major improvements can cost tens of thousands of dollars and take months to complete. Regardless o what you plan, you must estimate these cost to determine whether a deal makes sense. The cost of rehab represents a major portion of your project's overall expense. In some cases, the market will not support the cost of the repairs and improvements and still return a decent profit.

Costs of Sale: At the close of escrow, certain costs of the transaction are apportioned to the buyer and seller. For example, title insurance, taxes, fees, and costs, average 2% of the sales price are commonly charged to the seller.

Realtor's commission. Don't let the 5 or 6% commission that an agent charges to list your house for sale scare you off from hiring an agent. Studies show that a skilled Realtor can sell a home in half the time it takes homeowners to sell it themselves and the higher sales price more than covers their commission. So, overall, you are likely to save on holding costs and command a higher sales price at the same time if you utilize a realtor. In addition, you have more time to find, buy, rehab, and flip your next property.

Here's another secret: Don't forget to factor in the value of your time and effort. After all, flipping also involves your time: finding deals, negotiating with sellers, evaluating deals, doing your due
diligence, completing the purchase, making repairs and improvements, working with your dream
team. The entire process takes a lot of time, and your time has value! So when you're evaluating
a deal, first determine whether you have the time to devote to the project, and then whether the
 return you expect is worth your time.

Secret 44

Consult with Your Dream Team Before Buying

Here's a simple rule of thumb: Only deal with people you trust. (Why would you ever deal with someone you don't trust?) If, for example, a contractor you asked for estimated repair costs for a house, goes around you and contacts that homeowner directly (or bids on that house at the foreclosure auction), never deal with that contractor again. It's that simple! Real professionals make money helping you, not stealing deals. (But at the same time, don't be paranoid. Spending your time being secretive is a waste of effort.)

When you are first starting out, put together a "Dream Team" of professionals to work with you. You should always be the least experienced person on your Dream Team. As long as these professionals have more experience that you, you're in good company. In that way, you'll always be learning.

Your attitude should be to learn everything they already know. You can sort out their suggestions and advice later; put some of it to good use, and ignore the recommendations you don't value. But always keep in mind that more people will share information with you as long as you treat them with integrity, show a sincere interest in learning, and demonstrate that you appreciate their opinions.

If a member of your Dream Team seems really interested in one of your properties, consider going partners on the deal. You'll spread your risk, leverage your skills, and develop a closer working relationship with that person. And that relationship will build trust and ultimately create a stronger team.

Secret 45

Don't Let "Buyer's Panic" Affect You

Have you ever heard of *"Buyer's Panic"*? Buyer's panic sneaks in when you think a deal is too good to be true and you don't want it to lose it. Typically you'll experience this sensation when the homeowner reneges on the deal or another investor offers them a better deal. You'll also experience buyer's panic at a foreclosure auction when the bidding rises above your maximum bid.

No matter how much time you spend evaluating a deal, talking with homeowners, working through issues, negotiating with lienholders, and planning renovations and repairs, in the end your only concern should be whether you can make a reasonable profit when you flip the house. If you can't, it doesn't matter how much time you spend, it's not a good deal.

Good flippers are rational and objective, checking their emotions at the door. You need to develop the same thick skin. Be professional, be courteous, and be considerate, but don't get emotional. Remember, your "wins" and "losses" are determined when you calculate your profits after you flip a house, not when you buy it.

It is easy to become emotional dealing with distressed homeowners. Although you are encouraged to empathize with homeowners who are under duress, don't get emotionally involved. Lifeguards are careful to remember that drowning people can take them under, too. Similarly, you want to save the homeowners from experiencing any more pain without having them take you under. Inform them of their options, offer them a fair deal, but don't give away your profits trying to help them. Always keep in mind that this is a business deal, and good deals benefit both parties, which includes you.

If the homeowner changes his mind about selling, or receives a better offer, don't get emotional. Re-evaluate the situation, and either offer more money (if you can still make a profit) or walk away. Don't let buyer's panic affect you. If the bidding at the foreclosure auction exceeds your max bid, walk away! In all of these situations, you'll be thankful later.

Section G: Financing

Secret 46

The House Doesn't Need to be in Good Condition to be Financed

The condition of the house is only one of several factors lenders will consider when deciding whether to approve a loan. In fact, loan approval is like a jigsaw puzzle; all the pieces must fit. A poorly maintained house may still fit perfectly with the rest of the pieces of your puzzle. So, even for a house in poor condition, there are still loans available depending on other factors.

What are those factors? Well, from a lender's point of view, a borrower who demonstrates both the *"ability"* and the *"willingness"* to repay the loan is a good risk, regardless of the condition of the property. But how does the lender determine your "ability" to repay the loan? Lenders ask two basic questions about your ability to pay. First, is your income large enough to cover the expenses associated with the loan (less any existing debt obligations you have that will continue in the future)? Second, do you have enough cash to meet the up-front cash requirements of the purchase? (In other words, can you cover the down payment and closing costs?)

With respect to your "willingness" to repay the loan, lenders review your current financial situation, your past credit history, and your credit score. The way lenders see it, how you've handled credit in the past is the best indicator of how you'll handle credit in the future.

Other factors also come into play. One of the most important factors lenders evaluate is the loan-to-value ratio ("LTV"). This ratio is the percentage relationship between the amount to be borrowed and the appraised value of the property. For example, if you buy a house for $200,000, give a down payment of $50,000 and borrow $150,000, then the LTV is 75% ($150,000 divided by $200,000). Note: the more money you put down, the lower the LTV (which is better as far as lenders are concerned).

Why is the LTV ratio important to lenders? Because the lower the LTV, the less risk the lender faces, and consequently the more likely the lender will approve the loan. For example, if your credit is poor, the lender may require a lower LTV than for an individual with good credit.

Because the lender evaluates your ability to repay, your willingness to
repay, and the LTV ratio, among other factors, a house in poor condition still stands as good a chance for loan approval as a house in good condition, provided the other factors are within the lender's guidelines.

For example, you purchase a property that is well-maintained and in good condition. It has a fair market value of $200,000. You could probably get a loan for $160,000 (90% LTV). However, if it's in poor shape, and its value is closer to $150,000, you won't qualify for a $120,000 loan from a conventional lender. This is because the LTV ratio is extremely unfavorable. But if you can buy the property for $100,000 and finance only $50,000, the LTV would be 50% and the lender may happily approve the loan.

There are other programs available, too, such as an FHA 203(k) loan that can lend on future value. While this program is not open to flippers (unless HUD owns the property), this is a great way to get into a house and have the government finance (and insure) the rehabilitation!

Finally, if you're turned down for a loan, don't assume it is a bad thing. Think of it as getting a "second opinion." Perhaps the lender thought that the chance of making a profit on the flip would not be that great and has saved you from making a costly mistake. Take the rejection in stride and keep looking for better opportunities.

Secret 47

<u>Never Use All of Your Own Money to Buy Houses</u>

Using only your own funds is never a good idea! By using all of your own money, you gain no leverage. Wealth is created through leverage, so use leverage to your advantage. The amount of money you have access to limits the type of property you can afford to buy, thus limiting your maximum amount of profit. Further, using your own money unnecessarily exposes your personal assets to risk and may even compromise your potential tax savings (if you cash out retirement accounts, for example).

Of course, it is easy to understand why you may be reluctant to borrow from friends, family and/or investors. You don't want to risk losing someone else's money and having that person become upset with you. As a result, you may make some dubious decisions, like cashing-out the equity in your own home, cashing out your retirement accounts, or using your business as collateral for loans. Don't do this!

As a flipper, you should try to use as much of other people's money ("OPM") as possible. This would include borrowing from other investors, friends and family, traditional banks, and hard money lenders. By using other peoples' money, you'll not only be able to spread the risk, but also purchase larger properties, and increase your (and your partners') cash-on-cash return.

Another way to finance your transaction is to convince the seller's lender to finance your transaction. In other words, rather than obtaining your own financing to purchase a house, contact the homeowner's lender and see if they would allow you to assume the homeowner's current mortgage.

If the lender won't allow you to assume, you could still purchase the property *"subject to"* the existing mortgage. With subject to, you would simply take over the homeowner's monthly payments while you own the house. Then, when you flip the house, you'll pay off the balance of the mortgage.

Another financing opportunity arises when you buy a REO property directly from a lender. When you submit an offer to buy a REO, ask the lender to provide the financing. Some lenders may be willing to finance the purchase of the house, simply to divest itself of the property and get the bad loan off its books. Other lenders won't. But you won't know until you ask, and it never hurts to ask. The worse they could say is no.

Secret 48

You Don't Need Your Own Money to Buy Houses

If you find a house priced below market value with good flipping potential, you can always find sources of cash to help you make that investment. Even if you have very little or no money of your own! It may come from the seller, or the lender, or other investors. In other words, when you buy a house, you still need cash. It just doesn't have to be *your* cash.

For example, if you use the equity purchase strategy to acquire a house, you're only paying the homeowner a fraction of his equity; typically no more than $1,000 to $5,000. And if you don't have the cash yourself, there are several techniques you can use to get the money.

In contrast, if you use the equity split strategy, you're not going to pay the homeowner anything initially to purchase the house. They will be paid out of the proceeds when you eventually flip the house.

In other situations, the homeowners may carry the financing themselves, so you won't need to use your own money. In still other situations, the existing lender may be very willing to provide the financing for the purchase. And if nothing else works, you can always advertise for a partner (such as another investor like yourself) interested in financing the purchase in order to participate in a good deal. There are unlimited possibilities. You are limited only by your own imagination.

Keep in mind, your goal should be to leverage the power of other people's money (called "*OPM*"). By limiting the amount of cash you put in and maximizing the value of money you borrow, you will share some of your profits with your investors and/or lenders, but you'll also lower your risk and increase the rate of return on your investment.

Secret 49

<u>Flip Contracts (Not Houses)</u>

Good news! You don't need money or credit to buy properties. Nor do you need to take on the complicated process of repairing properties and then selling them. Instead, you can serve as a "bird-dog," finding and tying-up properties. Then, once you have those properties under contract, you can quickly turn around and flip the contract ("assign") to another flipper for a modest profit. In other words, instead of flipping properties, you can start out flipping contract.

Who are these investors? They are people eager to buy properties they can own or flip. But these investors don't know how to find them (or more precisely don't have the time to find them). Many are part-time flippers who hold full-time jobs. They have cash to invest and the resources to rehab a house, but they don't have the time to find and analyze the deals. This is where you come in. When you provide them with good deals, you and these investor both win.

What is the advantage of this approach? You don't spend time and money (money that you may not even have) buying properties or performing repairs. You simply make money finding great deals and assigning your contracts to other flippers. The disadvantage is that you won't make as much money on each deal. You could also find yourself tying-up a house that you can't find an investor to purchase from you. But those situations are far outweighed by the advantages if you don't have the money to invest or are just getting started.

Working with another flipper can take one of two basic forms. With the first approach, the flipper puts up the money and you find the deals. You'll purchase the house in his or her name and receive a fee for your efforts. With the second approach, you enter into a contract to purchase a house in your name, and then assign the contract to another flipper.

What is *"assigning"* the contract? Assigning a contract means another investor "buys" your contract for a fee. Once the contract is assigned, you receive a fee and are no longer involved in the transaction. The new owner of the contract is now the buyer of the property and enjoys all the rights conferred by that contract. The other party (the seller of the property) is still bound by the provisions of the contract.

But unless you have another investor or partner lined-up,

don't automatically assume you can flip a contract. Obstacles and roadblocks do pop up. Make sure you can afford to hold the house for at least 30 days, just in case.

Secret 50

You Can Assume or Take Subject to the Existing Loan

With some deals, you may be able to assume the existing loan, even if the homeowner is in default. As contradictory as it sounds, it is true! This is because the lender's decision to allow assumption is actually based upon other factors. Let's explore the confusing world of assumptions.

First, what is "**assumption**"? Assuming a loan simply means that you step into the shoes of the previous borrower and become personally liable to the lender for the repayment of the loan. You sign an assumption agreement and take over the owner's mortgage. You are now legally responsible for making the monthly mortgage payments.

Next, let's discuss which loans are assumable and which are not. Almost all FHA, VA, and adjustable rate mortgages ("ARMs") are assumable. Some conventional loans and subprime mortgages will also allow assumptions. To find out whether a particular mortgage is assumable, review the borrower's promissory note looking for language allowing assumption. If the note, mortgage, or deed of trust prohibit assumption the documents will contains a due-on-sale clause that states:

> *"If all or any part of the mortgaged property or an interest therein is sold or transferred by the borrower without the lender's prior written consent, the lender may, at the lender's option, declare all the sums secured by the mortgage to be immediately due and payable."*

What does this language mean? It doesn't mean the homeowner can't sell his property. What it does mean is that if he does sell (or in any way transfers ownership of) the property without the lender's consent, the lender has the right (but not the obligation) to call the whole loan due. In the alternative, the lender can require that the new owner assume the loan. What? Yes, you heard me right. A non-assumable loan is assumable. How is that possible? Let me explain.

If the non-assumable clause is in the note, mortgage, or deed of trust, you should contact the lender and make application to assume the loan. If you don't assume the loan (typically within 30 days), the lender has the right to accelerate the loan and demand the immediate repayment of the full loan balance. So, it's always better to attempt to assume the loan.

But why would you assume a loan rather than simply getting your own? Because the existing loan may have a lower interest rate than is currently available, or you may have an easier time qualifying for the loan, or you'll pay less closing costs. Finally, if you're in the process of assuming the loan, the lender may postpone the foreclosure auction so that your transaction can be finalized.

But why would a lender allow an assumption of a non-assumable loan? For any number of reasons:

1. As a condition to assumption, the lender will require you to reinstate the loan. Once that occurs, the lender won't have to foreclose. In that way, the lender avoids the hassle and expense of repairing the house, listing it, and selling it as an REO.

2. The interest rate on the existing mortgage is higher than current market rates, so the lender prefers keeping the existing loan in place.

3. You have already established a good business relationship with that lender and they would like to have you takeover another loan.

Bottom line: Never assume a mortgage unless it's in your best interest! Ask questions. Ask for help. Ask if you can assume a non-assumable loan. You just might be able to.

Secret 51

Develop Long Term Relationship with Lenders

If you're going to become a successful flipper, you'll need to develop a relationship with a lender. In fact, several lenders. Why? Because you'll need loans to buy houses. And because lenders want good deals to finance. They'd be crazy not to. But more importantly, lenders are looking for long-term relationships with clients. So rather than focusing on your one good deal, approach a lender about a long-term relationship. Explain that you are a new flipper and plan on buying and selling properties (which will require financing).

This is music to lenders' ears. After all, lenders want to establish solid business relationships with successful investors who buy and sell properties. They don't want just one isolated deal. Similarly, you should want to establish a solid business relationship with a good lender. Accordingly, when you are first starting out, and you have no track record, it will help for you to show the lender that you know what you're doing. If you run into a problem, try this approach: Find a house in your area and write-up a brief business plan. In your plan, show the price you would pay for that property, how much you would finance, estimate how much it would cost to fix-up, what the after-repaired value will be when the your rehab is finished, how long it would take to sell, and your estimated profit (after paying off your financing). This will show the lender that you are able to plan ahead, are financially responsible, and know what you are doing, even if you don't end-up buying this particular house.

So how do you get started? Easy. Approach a lender (or mortgage broker) about getting *"pre-approved"* for a loan. Lenders are always interested in getting their clients pre-approved so that they can work with them in the future on their deals. But notice, I said "pre-approved," not "pre-qualified." Let's understand the difference before we proceed.

Pre-qualification simply means a lender has given an opinion about whether you qualify for a loan based upon what you told the lender about your financial condition. However, the lender did not review your financial documents or perform its own independent evaluation of your finances or credit report.

In contrast, ***pre-approval*** is much more involved and credible. Pre-approval means you have provided your lender with your tax returns, bank statements, 1099s and/or W-2s, and other documents the lender needs to evaluate your finances. Further, the lender has checked your credit report, and most of the documents needed for your loan have been analyzed.

All you're really waiting for at this point is a house, accepted contract, appraisal and title! Believe me, realtors, sellers, and asset managers will be more impressed with a pre-approval letter when they consider the credibility of your offer (in relation to other offers).

Once you have a solid track record showing that you have bought and sold several properties for a profit, lenders will be more willing to work with you. A good lender will also give you advice on how to improve your credit rating, improve your net worth, and gather up the documentation you need to satisfy underwriting requirements. A good lender will help you act quickly by evaluating your financial means, giving you advice, assessing your potential investment opportunities. While it will cost the lender time, good lenders see time spent working with you as an investment that will pay off as your flipping takes off.

Secret 52

Lenders Want To Do Business With You

Lenders need you. Without you, they don't exist. After all, they make money by lending to people just like you. A lender isn't doing you a favor by approving your loan. They're generating revenue through application fees, points, and the interest charged on your loan.

While it is true that lenders like to make large loans to major clients, their bread and butter is actually homeowners and small investors like you. By working with hundreds of thousands of clients they spread their risk and diversify their loan portfolios.

Flippers, just like you, are a great source of repeat business for lenders. A mortgage broker would love to make 2, 3, 4, or more loans to you each year. Let your mortgage broker know you plan to buy, rehab and flip properties and you're looking for a lending partner. If she doesn't seem interested, look elsewhere. There are dozens of mortgage brokers in your area who would love to do business with you.

In the interim, make yourself a more attractive borrower. Remember the old adage, *"banks only lend to people who don't need it."* While that adage is an exaggeration, there is a cornel of truth. You need to make your financial condition look as good as possible in the eyes of the lender. Then they will want work with you. Work on increasing your net worth (the total value of your assets minus your liabilities). Check your credit report regularly and correct any discrepancies. Pay your bills on time. Try to save some money. The more attractive you are as a borrower, the more money you can borrow and the less you have to pay to borrow it. Borrowers who represent a high level of risk pay dearly for it.

Secret 53

Use Hard Money Lenders When Needed

Let's say you find a house that you want to flip. It's a great deal, but the house needs major renovations. If you can fix it up, you can flip it for a substantial profit. The problem is that because of its condition, you can't get conventional financing. There is only one viable option: **Hard Money**.

What is hard money? A hard money loan is a high-interest, short-term loan. You can find hard money lenders (sometimes called "private money") through your mortgage broker, or from other investors in your area. You can also find them listed on the internet and in the real estate/loans classified section of your local newspapers. These lenders include private finance groups, local mortgage brokers, or just regular folks looking for a good place to park their money and yield high returns. Hard money offers you three major advantages:

1. You get access to financing you may not be able to get through a conventional lender.

2. Hard money lenders often accept the future value of a property as collateral. In that way, you don't have to borrow against your home or other assets. You

might even be able to borrow enough to cover both the purchase price and the cost of rehabbing the house.

3. You can set-up a separate escrow account with a hard money lender to fund repairs and renovations.

The major disadvantage of a hard money loan is its cost. That's why they call it HARD money. It's hard to pay back! Why is the interest rate so high? Because these lenders incur greater risk making these loans, and they want a commensurate return for that risk.

When dealing with a hard money lender, you can expect the following:

Interest Rate. Because of the higher risk, interest rates are correspondingly higher, sometimes double the going rate for conventional loans. For example, if the current rate for a fixed-rate mortgage is 6%, you can expect to pay between 12 and 14% for a hard money loan.

Points. Hard money lenders often require you to pay a fee ("points") for arranging the loan. The fee ranges between two to four points depending on the deal. One point equals 1% of the loan amount. For example, with a $100,000 loan at four points, you'll pay $4,000 just for the lender to arrange the loan.

Loan-to-Value Ratio. Loan-to-value ("LTV") is the ratio of the loan to the value of the property. For example, a loan of $100,000 on a house valued at $200,000 has an LTV of 50%. Hard money lenders will typically loan only 50 to 65% of the property's value (not the purchase price). So, depending on what you pay for the house, you may need additional funds to cover repairs and/or holding costs.

Term. The term of the hard money loan will be typically one year (rather than a typical 30 year loan). But because of the risk, the hard money lender will want you to pay the interest monthly. As a result, your monthly payment will be higher than with a conventional loan.

Balloon Payment. Many hard money loans have balloon payments. Instead of making equal payments over the life of the loan, the final payment is the remaining balance. If your loan is amortized over 10 years but is due in one year, you'll have a huge balloon payment when the loan comes due. If you line-up other financing in the meantime, or flip the house, that's not a problem. But if you don't, you'll need to have sufficient funds to handle the balloon payment.

Prepayment penalties. Because of the short-term nature of the loan, most hard money lenders waive the prepayment penalty if the loan is paid off sooner.

Closing costs. Hard money loans are closed just like conventional loans. You will be required to pay any fee or points you agree upfront, so make sure you fully understand your responsibilities at closing before you agree to the loan.

Does all of this sound scary? It can be if you don't take the time to understand the deal and what it means to your investment. Look at it this way, the profit the hard money lender makes is irrelevant. What matters is *your* profit. Simply factor the cost of financing into your calculations, just as you would repair costs, real estate commissions, or any other expense. After all, if you can make a decent profit on your flip, does it really matter how much the hard money lender makes on the deal? It really shouldn't matter, because you are still making your profit and you couldn't get a loan from a conventional lender. In other words, don't let the cost of the hard money loan blind you to the profits involved in the deal.

You should also take into consideration how long you'll need the loan. For example, the hard money lender is charging you 12% interest per year. But you only need the loan for four months (because you're going to renovate and then flip the house in four months), you're not really paying 12%. In that situation, the effective interest rate is only 4% for you (not 12%). That means that money is going to cost you only 4% for four months. If you look at that way, suddenly it doesn't sound so bad, especially when you consider you couldn't qualify for a conventional loan anyway.

Secret 54

Use Your Home Equity Loan to Purchase Properties

If you've paid down your mortgage, you could have enough equity in your home that a lender may consider a home equity loan. What is equity? *Equity* is the difference between your home's current market value and the outstanding loans encumbering it. For example, if your home is worth $200,000 and you only owe $150,000 on it, you have $50,000 equity.

If you do have equity, you can use that equity to finance the purchase of properties that you can fix and flip. You can also use your home equity funds to pay for repair and renovation costs once you own the property. There are no restrictions on how you use your loan proceeds. But before proceeding, understand that there are two ways to go:

    1. *Refinance your existing mortgage.* Let's say you own a $200,000 home and you owe only $100,000 on your existing mortgage. You could refinance by borrowing $150,000, of which $100,000 would be used to pay off the balance of your existing mortgage and the remaining $50,000 you could use to invest in properties. Notice that after the refinance, you would still have $50,000 equity remaining in your home as a safety net. Many people

choose this option, but there are at least two disadvantages. First, you'll pay closing costs on the new loan. Second, you now have higher mortgage payments (because you have a higher loan balance) which will continue for the life of the new loan. And if you had a lower interest rate with your existing mortgage, and market rates are trending higher, you'll lose that lower rate when you refinance.

2. **Home equity loan.** In contrast to a refinance, a home equity loan doesn't disturb your first mortgage. It is a new loan which is also secured by your home, but is in a junior position behind the existing mortgage. Obtaining a home equity loan doesn't require an extensive approval process because the risk to the lender is typically covered by the value of your home.

If you decide on a home equity loan, there are two subtypes; 1) home equity loan, and 2) home equity line of credit. The main difference is that proceeds from a home equity loan are distributed immediately. In other words, if you take out a $50,000 home equity loan, you get all of those funds immediately. Also, you start making payments on the full amount immediately.

In contrast, a home equity line is a line of credit up to a maximum amount, but you only pay for what you use. For example, if you take a $50,000 home equity line, that amount is available to you, but you don't have to draw all (or any) of it out until you're ready. You use it only when you need it. If you need only $10,000 today, you draw down that amount and make interest payments only that

$10,000 (not on the entire $50,000 as you would if you got a home equity loan). In other words, you only pay interest on the amount you are actually borrowing (not the amount on your note or deed of trust). And, at any time, you can increase or decrease the amount you are using.

As a result, a home equity line is almost always the better choice, because even if you'll eventually need to use the entire available line of credit, you can delay your spending appropriately to avoid unnecessary interest payments. Plus, as you pay down your equity line, you can withdraw from the available balance as many times as you like. Most importantly, you'll leave your senior loan undisturbed, which means you can continue to take advantage of the lower interest rate and payments on that loan.

But there are also disadvantages. Because the line of credit is more flexible and convenient that a home equity loan, you will pay a higher interest rate. Also because values have fallen dramatically in the past years and are now slowly recovering, lenders are much stricter about values and are not issuing lines of credit as they once did.

Even if you don't need a home equity line of credit to invest in properties, we strongly recommend that you apply for a line of credit anyway. A line of credit gives you a buffer in the event that cash flow becomes a problem. You can draw down from your line at any time and then simply pay the money back when you get it. Sure, you'll pay some interest on the money you draw out, but if you pay it back quickly, the interest is usually minimal and is tax-deductible as mortgage interest.

Section H: Auctions

Secret 55

Foreclosure Auctions Are Great For Finding Houses

Foreclosure sales are held in publicly accessible locations, typically outside county buildings. The old stereotype of an auction on the courthouse steps is still true. If the notice of foreclosure refers to the sale being held on the courthouse steps, it literally means the steps outside the courthouse. Even if it is raining, the sale will still be conducted outside!

You probably won't be alone on the steps. If there is equity in the property, expect others bidders to be present and eager to bid. At other times, nobody shows up! If that occurs, you can assume the house is worth less than the balance owed the foreclosing lender.

Rules and regulations vary state to state. In most states, like California, you'll need to have cash (or cashier's checks) for the total amount of the purchase price of the property. It is best to bring several cashier's checks for various amounts so that you are prepared for any eventuality. In other states, you only need 5-10% and you've got 30 days to pay the balance. (Check with your state's laws to leanr what is required.)

Prepare for last-minute postponements, because they are

common. The foreclosure could be resolved or postponed at the last minute for a variety of reasons (i.e. the homeowners reinstating the loan, filing for bankruptcy, or filing a complaint with the court to enjoin the sale). You can always call the trustee's or sheriff's office the morning of the sale or check their website to confirm the auction is still on.

The auction begins with a recital of the property address. The person conducting the sale is called the *"auctioneer."* After the introduction and the property address, the sale begins.

The opening bid is always made by the foreclosing lender. This bid is called the lender's "*credit bid*." The credit bid is the total amount owed the lender, including the mortgage balance, late payment charges, taxes, insurance advanced by the lender, and any other costs incurred by the lender. The credit bid is, in essence, an indication of what the lender needs to get from the sale of the house in order to breakeven.

Remember, as the creditor, the lender carries no responsibility for maintenance, repair, upkeep, or other costs until it acquires title to the house. So if the lender knows of major problems with the house, it may under bid to make sure someone else buys it. As long as the lender doesn't actually own the property, the lender is just another interested party. But once the lender owns the property (which it will if no one else bids higher), then it assumes all the responsibilities for repairing the problems and the costs of ownership.

If the lender underbids, you may not want the house unless you have inside knowledge. For example, you may have been able to inspect the house and determined that what appeared at first glance to be a major foundation problem is actually a minor cosmetic issue. The problem is, as you've probably guessed, you may not know whether the lender under-bids because they know of the problem or are just eager to get rid of the property, or both. That's why attending several foreclosure auctions as an observer first will help give you a sense of what actually happens at the auction before you become a real bidder.

Lenders credit bid for the amount they are owed. If the winning bid is for a greater amount than the lender's credit bid, the remaining funds, or surplus monies, go to junior lienholders, if any. Then, if any money is left, and there rarely ever is, it goes to the homeowner (who has the right to claim the remainder). However, very seldom will there be surplus monies. Bidders are looking for great deals and want to pay significantly less than market price for the house. So any equity the homeowner thought they had, will quickly evaporate at the foreclosure sale.

Frequently the amount of the lender's credit bid is higher than what investors are willing to pay and/or the market value of the house. If no one else bids and the lender is the sole and only bidder, the lender becomes the owner of the property. In that event, the property is referred to as an "*REO*" (real estate owned by the lender). Under Federal banking laws, the lender is required to sell the property as soon as possible. So, even though the house you wanted reverted to the foreclosing lender at the foreclosure auction, the lender doesn't want to keep the property. They want to sell it as quickly as possible so that they can get it off their books (it's a liability to them). If you find yourself in this situation, you should contact the lender's REO department as soon as possible after the foreclosure sale, and submit an offer to purchase the house.

Here's another secret: If a third party investor is the highest bidder, they are also often eager to flip the house as quickly as possible for a profit. In that case, you can still make a good deal by approaching the investor and offering to buy the house immediately *"as is."* This is a "win/win" situation and investors love it!

Secret 56

Attend Auctions and Bid on Houses

Foreclosure auctions are open to the public. Anyone can attend. So although professional buyers attend these auctions, you also have the legal right to attend. And you don't have to do anything to exercise that legal right. You don't need reservations or a ticket. Simply show-up at the courthouse steps and you're there! The time, location, and other details of these auctions are listed in the notices of sale. You can find these notices recorded in the county recorder's office and published in your local newspaper. Once you're there, no one will try to stop you from attending, and no one will ask you for proof that you have a right to be there. In fact, no one will even care unless you draw attention to yourself.

Although anyone can attend the auction, not everyone can "bid." Many states have had problems in the past with bidders not following through on their purchases. As a consequence, many states have enacted rules many years ago that prevent just anyone from bidding.

Now, before the sale begins, the auctioneer will require that bidders "*qualify*" to bid. How do you qualify? In order to qualify, you will need to show the auctioneer that you have cashier's checks equal to the maximum amount you plan on bidding. At that point, you have been qualified and will be permitted to bid on the property. Make sure you know these rules before you bid. In order to understand auction procedures, go to as many auctions as you can, even if you're not interested in any of the properties. Each time you attend, you'll get a better feel for the process and for the regulars who usually attend.

Over time, you'll also develop a sense of what's a good price. This is important because a house in foreclosure will almost always sell for 20-30% less than it would if it were sold on the open market. Checking out properties for sale and then attending the auctions will help you develop the ability to calculate foreclosure values from an flipper's point of view. And it's a free education, because the auctions are open to the public.

So, what are you waiting for? Attend some auctions!

Secret 57

It Doesn't Matter How Many People Bid At the Auction

Sometimes the only person attending the auction will be the auctioneer. Not even the foreclosing lender will attend. On other occasions, a few other people will attend, but they won't necessarily bid.

Besides, how many people attend the foreclosure auction is irrelevant. All you should care about is whether you can get the house at a price you can make a profit when you flip. You can purchase great properties when you're the only person in attendance. You can also attend jam-packed auction where the lender's opening bid was higher than the value of the property and nobody bids.

In actuality, the number of investors who show-up to bid is a function of the property's value in relation to the lender's opening bid. Remember; the foreclosing lender always bids first. If the lender's opening bid is **greater** than the market value of the house, no one will attend the sale and/or bid. If no one else bids, the lender receives the property in lieu of the loan being paid off. The property is now referred to as *"Real Estate Owned"* by the lender or simply *"REO."*

But what happens if the lender's opening bid is **less** than the value of the house? Then there will be lots of bidders in attendance eager to buy the property. And everyone present can bid, including you!

For example, let's say a house has a value of $200,000. If the foreclosing lender's opening bid is $250,000 (the amount they are owed), then no one will bid. Why would they? Nobody wants to spend $250,000 for a house that's only worth $200,000. If no one else bids, the house will go to the foreclosing lender (the only bidder) and will become an "REO." But what if the lender's opening bid is only $100,000? In this situation, there is approximately $100,000 equity in this property, so it is potentially a good deal (if it can be purchased right). In this scenario, it is likely several investors will attend the auction eager to bid.

In preparation, you should attend as many foreclosure auctions as you can. Consider them as dress rehearsals or practice sessions. After you've attended a few, you'll get a sense for how the "lookie-lou's" and the "professionals" like to bid and how to distinguish between them. Lookie-lou's are people who frequent these auctions because they are "free entertainment" in the same way people attend court hearings. Some of them may even bid on a property once at the very beginning of the auction, just for the sheer thrill of bidding. Others in attendance are professionals and know exactly what they are doing. They are easy to spot. They usually have cellphones hanging out of their ears and/or clipboards overflowing with notes. Watch them carefully. Some only want properties if they can win at rock-bottom prices. They'll quickly stop bidding once the price reaches a certain level. Others won't bid until all the casual bidders have given up and stopped bidding. They try to conceal their interest in the property until the very last minute. Don't be fooled by this behavior. If they weren't interested in the house, they wouldn't have attended the auction in the first place.

Once you plan on attending an auction to actually bid, be sure you are prepared. Have a folder for each property you're intending to' bid on and cashier's checks equal to the amount necessary to pay for the property (should your bid be the highest). Most importantly, before the bidding starts on a property, review your notes and recommit yourself to not bidding above your "walk-away price."

While you will learn to spot the lookie-lou's and professionals, remember that in the end it doesn't matter how many people attend the auction. A good investment is a good investment, and a bad investment is a bad investment.

Secret 58

You Need a Strategy When Bidding at the Auction

Many bidders at auctions do not stay rational and let their emotions get the best of them. If that's the case, a little gamesmanship can be the difference between winning and losing a property. Also, if a competing bidder bids too much for a property, he may not have the funds to compete against you when the next auction rolls around.

But before you even think about bidding, you need a "dress rehearsal." Research several properties scheduled for auction and prepare a detailed portfolio for each one, complete with your walk-away price. (Your walk-away price is the highest price you will pay for this particular property.) Now attend the auction for those houses and observe what happens. Was your price too high? Too low? Did the bidding exceed your walk-away price? Were you on target with the price you would have been willing to pay?

You might also consider following-up with the investor who purchased the house to see how much money the investor sunk into the project, and what the house ultimately sold for (assuming, of course, that person is willing to share this information).

In preparation for the auction, set your walk-away price and don't bid above that number no matter what! Once you've determined your walk-away price, the strategy you use when bidding during an auction depends on your personality and your ability to outfox your competition. Here are some techniques you can try:

+ ***Bid first and often.*** Nothing is more unnerving than a bidder who starts the bidding and continues bidding. This can discourage other bidders and cause them to stop bidding.

+ ***Wait to the very end to start bidding.*** You can wait until the very end of the auction when the auctioneer starts saying "Going once, going twice" and then start bidding. This is also unnerving to other bidders who thought they had the bidding all to themselves.

+ ***Bore the opposition into submission.*** Outbid the highest bidder by the minimum amount allowed. For example, the auctioneer may specify that bids must be in $50 increments. If so, keep bidding $50 higher than the previous bid. The other bidders may get bored, or irritated, and walk away.

+ ***Jump in the deep end.*** You can also open with an extremely high bid to try to shock your competition. You may be able to scare off an inexperienced bidder or two.

However, be careful because you may pay a lot more than necessary for the house. The bidding may never have reached the amount you bid. If you feel sure the house will sell for a lot more than your high opening gambit, give it a try. But never open with your maximum bid.

+ *Be Quiet and Mysterious*. Softly spoken and seemingly casual bids can give the impression of confidence and mystery. Some bidders may not even hear your bid, causing them to waste time and energy figuring out who you are and what you're up to.

+ *Be over the top*. You can holler your bids out so everyone in the area knows your offer. It's unsettling for other bidders to hear someone screaming at an auction. (But if you're shy or self-conscious, this may not be the strategy for you.)

Secret 59

Avoid "Buyer's Panic" at the Auction

House flippers come from all walks of life and backgrounds. Some flippers, like you, will approach the process rationally and objectively, seeking to minimize risk while maximizing their return. They appreciate that some of the best houses for flipping come from foreclosure auctions. Others will try to be rational, but will occasionally fail, especially at a foreclosure auction.

Foreclosure sales are auctions, and by their very nature are very competitive. Only one party wins the auction, and everyone else loses. This competitive nature leads to a variety of emotions. Attend an auction and watch the faces of bidders. You'll see fear, anxiety, excitement, apprehension, and even panic (or anger) when a bidder feels a property is slipping away.

Some houses are great investment opportunities, and a number of people will bid. In fact, the more people there interested, the higher the bidding will go. And then there are other houses which are poor investments, and yet a number of people will still bid.

Why is this so? It's called *"buyer-panic."* Buyer's panic occurs when a bidder thinks a particular house is the investment of a lifetime. He'll never get another chance at such an amazing opportunity. But when he sees the property slipping away, buyer's panic sets in, and he bids too high. Others may also fall under the spell of buyer's panic, or may simply think, *'Wow, he's bidding higher and higher. He must know something I don't know. I can't let this property slip away!"* Buyer's panic typically breeds further competition between bidders and causes the price to spiral further out of control.

The supply of properties is limitless! You are under no pressure whatsoever to buy any particular house, no matter how much time and effort you've put into investigating the deal. If you're interested in a house, due your due diligence and calculate your walk-away price. If you've done your homework, you'll never overbid. Employ any bid strategy you like at the auction and, no matter how many people bid, never bid higher than your walk-away price.

Any time the bidding goes past your walk-away price, stop bidding and take the time to watch the drama of emotions on the other bidders' faces. You'll be surprised what you'll learn about the emotional aspect of auctions - especially about what not to do.

Remember, the higher the bid, the lower the profit potential when you flip, and the higher the risk. You make your profit when you buy a house. If you pay too much, (thinking you will make-up the difference when you sell), you will be making a costly mistake. But buy at the right price, and you'll have a much better chance of earning a profit when it comes time to flip.

Secret 60

Don't Expect Immediate Possession After the Auction

If you're the highest bidder at the foreclosure auction, you become the owner of the house. You will receive a deed confirming you're the new legal owner, which will be recorded in the County Recorder's Office. But even though you're the owner, you still may not be entitled to immediate possession. Whether you are entitled to possession, will depend on whether the house is vacant or occupied. If it is vacant, no problem. You can take possession immediately, change the locks, and begin your rehab. However, if the house is still occupied, possession will depend on whether the house is occupied by the former owner or tenants. Let's approach each of these possibilities separately.

A. *Former Homeowners.* If the former homeowners are still occupying the house after the auction, you must serve them with a *"3-Day Notice to Quit."* They then have three days to voluntarily vacate. Hopefully they will. If they don't, you will need to file an unlawful detainer to have them evicted. You can do this yourself or you can hire an attorney that specializes in unlawful detainers (which is what I recommend). The eviction process takes approximately 4-6 weeks. Once you have obtained a court judgment for possession, the sheriff will conduct the physical eviction. Once the former owners are removed, you should immediately change the locks and take possession.

    B. *Tenants*. If there are tenants occupying the property, your approach should be slightly different. First, introduce yourself as the new owner to the tenants. Then determine whether they have a valid lease. If there is a period of months remaining on the lease, the best policy is to allow the tenants to remain in possession provided they start paying rent to you. If they don't have a valid lease, serve them with a *"60-Day Notice to Quit"* (or notice as required by your local rent control ordinance, if any). Hopefully, they will then voluntarily vacate the house. If they don't, follow the same eviction procedures as discussed above.

During this time, even though you don't yet have possession, you still have certain responsibilities as the new owner:

    Insure the property. You should immediately purchase property insurance for your new house. If the house is damaged or destroyed during this period, and you don't have insurance, you could lose your investment. Don't be surprised if the rates are slightly higher. Rates for insuring an investment property are higher than rates for an owner-occupied home because the insurance company's risk is higher. This is because owner-occupants tend to take better care of a house than a renter or an "ex-owner" remaining in the house.

Pay property taxes. As the new owner, you are now responsible for paying the property taxes until you flip the house. If you fail to pay the property taxes, the tax collector can sell a tax lien to collect the money owed, which means you'll also pay late fees and penalties. If another investor buys the tax lien, you could lose your investment if it isn't paid.

Keep an eye on the property. Try to protect it from vandalism or theft. Some homeowners (or tenants) may vindictively damage the house before they vacate. Or worse, they'll try to remove items that should remain when they leave, like cabinets, plumbing and electrical fixtures. If you notice anything suspicious, call the police.

Make necessary repairs. Necessary repairs are repairs to defects that make the house unsafe or could lead to further damage or deterioration. For example, fixing a leaky roof would be a necessary repair. In contrast, repainting the house (before you have possession) would not be.

Don't make unnecessary renovations. Remember; don't make any renovations to the house until you have physical possession. You could lose your investment if the former owners/tenants trash the house on their way out. In other words, you can make necessary repairs, but no renovations or improvements. Save your rehab until after the homeowners (or tenants) have vacated and you have physical possession.

If you find yourself with former owners or tenants who won't leave, you should be proactive. Here is one suggestion: Offer the them money in exchange for possession and their keys. This is called *"cash for keys."* In effect, yon offer the homeowners, for example, $1,000 if they will give you the keys and vacate the house immediately. Structure the agreement so you don't give them any money until the house is "broom-clean" and their moving van is in the driveway. And, if you do make an agreement, do it as early in the process as possible rather than near the end.

Here's another secret: While the unlawful detainer is pending, the homeowners have been known to quietly abandon the property, leaving the house vacant. Typically, they won't disclose they are leaving, slipping out in the middle of the night or over the weekend. So you will need to remain vigilant to this possibility. The courts are well aware that vacant houses tend to attract criminals and other riff-raff, so they'll speed up the process. If this should occur, advise your eviction attorney right away, so that he can advise the court and expedite the judgment for possession.

Section I: REOs

Secret 61

<u>REOs are a Great Source for Houses</u>

When most people consider flipping houses, they envision bidding on properties at auctions. They think the homeowner can't pay, so the lender takes the house and places it on the auction block. The fact is that the foreclosure process offers opportunities at several different stages to buy houses, including before, during, and after the auction.

In fact, some flippers specialize in purchasing houses at a specific stage in the foreclosure process. For example, some flippers prefer only pre-foreclosures. They prefer working directly with homeowners. Others do not enjoy interacting with homeowners and choose to wait until the auction. Still others focus exclusively on REO properties, preferring to work directly with lenders (or with the lender's real estate agent). For the most part, you should stay open to purchasing properties at any stage in the process as long as the deal makes sense.

The least understood of these three approaches is buying REOs directly from the lenders. So let's focus on that strategy. Buying REO properties offers a number of advantages for flippers like you. Consider this: Buying during the pre-foreclosure phase requires dealing with homeowners who are under a great deal of stress and financial pressure. Lenders, on the other hand, are professional operations, keeping normal office hours and following reliable procedures. There is no emotion involved. Lenders are motivated to sell the properties for business reasons. The only pressure they're under is federal guidelines to sell these properties quickly.

Lenders are eager to turn these liabilities (REOs properties) into assets by selling them and getting them off their books. Lenders want to hold mortgages, and receive payments, not spend money on maintenance, insurance, taxes, and the cost of selling properties. As a result, lenders often will offer incredible deals on their REO properties. One of the biggest reasons they're able to do so is due to property mortgage insurance (called "PMI").

Lenders require homeowners to purchase PMI when they finance more than 80% of the value of the house. The homeowner pays the premium even though the insurance covers the lender's risk. PMI protects lenders against potential losses in the event of borrower default. Specifically, PMI covers the loss if the lender sells a house for less than the balance of the loan.

As a result, the lender has little incentive to maximize the price it gets for the house, since ultimately the PMI must make up the difference between the sale price and the loan balance. In most cases, while it may sound harsh, the lender simply wants to unload the house.

One of the advantages of buying REO properties directly from the lenders is that you can fully inspect the houses before buying. This is because, in most cases, the lender has already evicted the previous owner (if they didn't voluntarily vacated the property). The lender now owns the property, so the lender can show it at any time. Remember, the biggest unknown involved in buying a house at the auction is the interior condition of the house, since you typically can't get inside to inspect the interior before the sale. But, with REO properties, you can inspect the house, both exterior and interior. Plus, you can bring a contractor in to provide an estimate. In that way, you'll create a detailed and accurate estimate of the cost and time required to make repairs and return the house to marketable condition. In other words, with an REO, you can make a very educated assessment of the flipping potential of that house.

How do you find out RE0 properties? There are two basic ways to locate REO properties: 1) through the lender, or 2) through real estate agents. Let's explore each method.

1. Lenders. Most lenders have departments responsible for selling their inventory of REO properties. Some lenders even have property management departments responsible for the maintenance and upkeep of their REO inventory. To find properties through lenders, call the lender and ask to speak to an asset manager in their REO department.

2. Realtors. The other method to find REO properties is to call real estate agents. Certain Realtors specialize in listing REOs, having established a business relationship with lenders. But caution, buying through an agent can raise the price you ultimately pay for the house. After all, the agent is responsible to the lender to get market price for the home. Also, the Realtor is motivated to sell for the highest price possible because their commission is based upon the sales price. So, you will typically make a better deal with the REO department rather than through a realtor.

Many real estate agents are eager to sell REO to flippers like you. This is because in most cases, flippers intend to resell the houses after making repairs and upgrades. So, if your agent sells you the house, she may also gain the listing when you're ready to flip it. A good real estate agent is eager to find flipper clients who provide a steady source of listings. A smart agent is also eager to sell REOs in the hopes of establishing exclusive listing arrangements with lenders. In that way, earning the right to list all the lender's REO properties.

Unfortunately, few lenders provide the financing for you to purchase their REO properties. So when you are first starting out, you are probably better off securing your own financing in advance from another lender before approaching a lender to buy an REO. This is called getting *"pre-approved."* In this way, you finance the first few properties and prove that you can do a good job with them.

Once you're well established and have built a strong relationship with lenders, you can perhaps pitch them on the idea of financing future REO acquisitions.

Secret 62

Buy REOs Directly From Lenders

Let's start with an understanding that lenders are in the loan business, not property management business. They want to make loans and, in return, collect payments and fees. Lenders don't want to be in the real estate business. In fact, they're legally prohibited from being in the real estate management business. As a result, when they get an REO property, they want to get rid of it as quickly as possible. So when you suggest that you can't get an REO directly from the lender, you are probably falling into one of three common traps.

First, don't deal with realtors (unless you have to). Now don't get me wrong, I love Realtors! Realtors are invaluable members of your Dream Team. They provide important functions to flippers, just not when buying REOs. The problem is that as a new flipper, you'll see the signs and advertisements for *"REO properties"* and *"bank-owned sales"* and rush after those properties. But you'll soon be frustrated when you discover the prices are too high and they're really not good deals. You see, here is the problem. Once a realtor obtains an REO listing from a lender, they will most likely list the house at (or slightly below) market value. Well, that's not good enough for you. You're looking for houses substantially below market (i.e. wholesale). As a result, you're always almost better dealing directly with lenders (unless the lender demands that you deal with their listing agent).

Second, don't buy at private auctions. These aren't foreclosure sales. These are private auctions where companies conduct monthly auctions to sell hundreds of bank-owned REOs. Now the problem with these auctions is that the people who attend and bid on these properties typically don't know what they're doing. They'll bid up a property to an unrealistic value, sometimes above its current market value! Once again, this is no deal. You buy wholesale, not retail. Forget these private auctions.

Third, buy from assets managers. With each property, there is only one asset manager in the lender's REO department authorized to sell that property. That is the ideal person you should be dealing with. Only that person can give you a substantial discount. The trick is to find those asset managers and contact them <u>before</u> they list the house with a realtor. The only exception would be when the asset manager has already listed with a realtor and requests that you deal with that realtor directly.

Now, let's consider the assets managers you're going to be dealing with. When negotiating with them, you have three strategies with respect to making offers. Let's look at each of these strategies separately.

1. ***Single* Offer**. The most common way to bid on REOs is to submit an offer for one property at a time. Find a house you're interested in and make an offer. Negotiate with the asset manager in the REO department of the lender (or the listing agent). In essence, it's like a normal real estate transaction between a buyer and seller, except in this case, the seller is the lender. In all other respects, it's really the same as dealing with any other seller. You can request the same contingencies as any other transaction, including inspection requirements, financing, and so forth.

If you're new to buying REOs to flip, a single offer on a single property is the best way to go. Bidding on individual houses one at a time will give you experience both in the buying process and, if your bid is accepted, in the process of repairing, renovating, and flipping.

When making offers on REOs, make sure you always include the provision that your offer is *"contingent on obtaining acceptable financing."* Doing so benefits you in two ways: (a) If you can't obtain financing, you are released from the contract, and (b) the REO lender may decide to offer financing to you at more favorable terms in order to speed-up the close of escrow.

   2. ***Multiple Offers*.** As an alternative to making one offer at a time, you can submit multiple offers on different properties simultaneously using separate contracts. The advantage to this approach is clear. Typically there are several REO properties you're interested in purchasing. If you use the single offer approach, you will submit an offer

for one property and start to negotiate with the asset manager. But what if while you are negotiating for that one house, another one (you were also interested in) sells. To avoid this problem, submit separate contracts on multiple properties. This will allow you to "hedge your bets" and expand your purchase opportunities.

The multiple offers strategy also creates some risk, especially if you can't afford to purchase them all. For example, if all the contracts are accepted, you have a dilemma because you can only afford to purchase one. Here are two ways to avoid this predicament.

The first is simply to make all your offers "contingent" on obtaining suitable financing. Let's say you submit contracts on three separate houses, but you can qualify to buy only one. If qualifying for financing on only one house is all you're eligible for, the other two contracts will be invalidated. (Effectively you've ensured you won't have to purchase all three, even though you bid on all three.)

But there's also a problem with that strategy. Your goal is to establish long-term relationships with asset managers so you'll receive advance notice of REO properties for sale (before they are listed with realtors). You'll also want to establish yourself as a credible and reputable buyer. This will help you during negotiations or when you're competing with another investor for a house. But here's the problem. The REO department will be irritated with your multiple offers since they may have stopped marketing the houses you didn't end-up buying. In other words, creating a financing contingency on multiple properties (you have no ability to purchase) may be an effective short-term technique, but may hinder you in the long run, and may alienate asset managers.

A better method of making multiple offers is to be upfront about your intentions with the asset manager when you make your offers. Include a contingency stating you're making offers on, for instance, three different houses, but you'll only be willing to purchase one of the three. To protect yourself, you can also include a contingency for obtaining financing for that house. In this way, the lender knows in advance that you aren't interested in purchasing all three. They'll appreciate your honesty and they'll understand why you're making multiple bids. And you'll create a positive, professional impression that will help establish a long-term business relationship for the future.

3. *One Offer on Multiple Properties.* Some flippers create investment groups made up of multiple investors. They pool their assets for the purpose of buying REO properties ("bulk purchases"), rehabbing and then flipping. If you (or your partners) have the financial resources, you can make a *blanket* offer to purchase a group of REO properties from a lender. The major advantage to this approach is that you're likely to pay a lower price per house when you buy all of the houses than you would if you had purchased them individually. Why? The lender may be delighted to dispose of a bulk of properties and therefore willingly reduce the total price. Plus, the more houses you purchase, the lower the risk you face of any one house

requiring extensive repairs and investment. In effect, you spread your risk like you would by diversifying stock market investments.

Regardless of which strategy you use, you always want to negotiate from a position of strength. In order to strengthen your position as a flipper you should have; 1) cash, or access to it, and 2) a pre-approval letter from a credible lender, before presenting your offer. Also, do what you say you're going to do, and know what you want before you ask for it. Asset managers do not have time to waste on people who simply want to test the waters and pretend to be investors.

Also, be sensitive to the needs of the asset manager. Asset managers have a duel problem they need to resolve: a bad loan and a house they don't want. Your job is to solve their problem and make a good deal in the process.

The REO process may take longer than a normal transaction, and there is good reason for this. You're dealing with a corporation, with multiple levels of responsibilities. Asset managers are required to report the various stages of negotiations to their superiors in order to show they did everything possible to get the best price. Accepting your first bid will not create the perception that the asset manager is a tough negotiator. That's another reason to expect your early offers to be denied.

Here's another secret. If your offer is initially rejected, you should request that your offer be kept on file as a *"back-up offer."* Lenders often reject offers that come early in the process in hopes of receiving higher offers later. But when the higher offers don't arrive or fall through during escrow, don't be surprised if that asset manager goes back to your back-up offer and accepts it.

Secret 63
Government REOs Are Good Deals

You can find great deals on government-owned houses, if you know where to look and who to talk to. The Federal Housing Administration ("FHA"), the Department of Veterans Affairs ("VA"), Internal Revenue Service ("IRS"), and other government agencies sell seized or surplus real estate on a regular basis. You can purchase government-owned properties through designated real estate agents, bidding at their auctions, and/or negotiating directly with the appropriate government agency. However, each agency has its own rules and regulations for sales. Some agencies contract with private companies to sell their properties, while others sell their properties themselves.

Federal Housing Administration. Let's start with FHA, a division of the Department of Housing and Urban Development ("HUD"). You may be wondering, how did FHA get these properties? The answer is simple. First-time homebuyers often finance their homes with FHA-insured loans. If the homeowner fails to make the mortgage payments, the FHA attempts to work with them to save their homes. If they can't, the FHA initiates foreclosure proceedings. Eventually, the FHA ends up with the properties and resells them through HUD-registered real estate agents.

FHA houses are typically lower-end properties because they were previously owned by first-time homeowners. Lower-end properties are easier to fix and flip than high-end properties. In addition, these houses will frequently sell for close to market value, so the chances of making huge profits are relatively low. Finally, FHA properties are sold *"as is"* without any warranties or representations (although you will be given the opportunity to make a complete inspection).

Keep in mind, FHA properties must be "owner-occupied" which complicates the fix and flip strategy. You'll be required to sign a contract stating you'll live in the house for at least 12 months before selling. As a result, if you're intent on flipping for quick profits, FHA properties are not for you. On the other hand, if you will commit to occupying the house for 12 months before you flip the house, you may qualify for FHA financing and possibly a low-interest loan (provided you are purchasing and renovating a rundown property). See www.HUD.gov for further details.

Department of Veteran Affairs. The VA also sells foreclosed properties. Repossessed VA properties are resold on the open market by VA-registered real estate agents. While you don't have to be a military veteran to purchase a house from the VA, you will need to agree to live in the house for 12 months. See www.va.gov for further details. In order to purchase as an "owner-occupied buyer" from the VA, some investors have been known to misrepresent their intentions and claim they fully intend to live in the home for the required 12-month period. We strongly discourage you from intentionally misrepresenting your situation. Government agencies check, and if they catch you in a lie, not only do you risk losing the house, but you can also face some stiff penalties and even jail time.

Internal Revenue Service. You can also buy properties from the IRS. The IRS is one of the most active government sellers of real estate because many homes are seized due to tax liens or tax defaults. IRS auctions are typically handled by mail. You can see houses for sale on the IRS website and get details about how to bid. If you are the winning bidder, you will need to submit 20% of the purchase price as a down payment, with the balance due within 30 days. But caution, the homeowners have four months to redeem the property. For further information: www.treas.gov/auctions/irs

Another IRS opportunity occurs when a lender forecloses on a house which has an IRS lien already recorded against it. The IRS lien always has priority. So when a property is foreclosed on, the IRS has the right to redeem the property or release its lien. So whoever buys a property at a foreclosure sale must give the IRS 120 days notice in case the IRS wishes to redeem the property and sell it to recover the taxes owed. The IRS has the right to take possession of the property, which means it will have to be sold at auction. Fortunately, the IRS does not normally do this. More commonly, the IRS will release their lien, but you need to request it in writing.

County Tax Collectors. Houses are also lost when homeowners fail to pay their property taxes. The taxing authority eventually seizes the house, sells it at auction, and uses the proceeds to recover the taxes owed. Tax sales are typically handled by the sheriff's office, county treasurer, or sometimes even the state. You can visit your county sheriff's office or treasurer's office for details on how the process works in your area.

Regardless, of which government agency you buy from, thoroughly inspect the property, use comparables (and your real estate agent) to determine its current value and after-repaired value, and do your due diligence. And keep this in mind; it doesn't have to be a government-owned property. Any deal you can profit on is a good deal. And, of course, if you don't think you can make a profit when you flip the house, walk away and wait for the next one!

Here are some other agencies you can also contact about properties they may have for sale:

1) US. Government Sales: www.homesales.gov/homes/homesforsale.cfm;
2) Federal Deposit Insurance Corporation: www.fdic.gov/buying/index.html,
3) Small Business Administration: www.sbc.gov/assets.html,
4) U.S. Customs: www.ice.gov
5) Treasury Dept: www.treas.gov/auctions/customs/realprop.html, and

6) USDA Real Estate For Sale: www.resales.usda.gov.

Section J: Rehabbing

Secret 64

Before You Begin Rehab, Clean the House

If you've purchased a house with the goal of fixing it and flipping it, you need to work quickly and do it right. Start with the "*Clean, Repair, Renovate*" philosophy. Clean it first. Then repair what doesn't work. Finally, renovate everything that needs updating. Your goal should be to get the house to market as quickly as possible. Obviously, the faster you can flip the house to market, the faster you can enjoy your profits.

First, replace the door locks as soon as you take possession. Do not wait, do it right away. I have had parties in my house, and I wasn't invited! Also check the window locks, garage door opener (if electric, change or reset the access code), and exterior lighting. Also, install a motion-detector floodlight in the front driveway.

Second, get a trash dumpster and clean up the exterior. Get rid of all trash, cut the lawn, cut back the shrubs, and give the house some curb appeal. Chances are that it has been neglected, and neighbors will be watching to see what's going on. This effort will make them feel good about you right away. The interior will probably have a lot of trash as well. Get several heavy-duty trash bags, and start filling them with everything in sight.

Next, power-wash the exterior completely. You can rent a power washer if necessary to get everything clean - the siding, concrete, windows, soffits, porches, garage doors. But don't use a power washer with too much pressure because you can damage wood and other porous surfaces easily, which will just add to your repair costs! It takes a minimum of 3500 PST pressure to remove years of dirt. Also, use one that has variable pressure tip attachments, and make sure it's gas powered, not electric.

Finally, you don't want a prospective buyer to say that the house has an unpleasant odor. Use some heavy-duty cleaner with a lemon or orange scent to give a fresh smell. Go to an industrial supply store and get the commercial strength cleaner. It will be well worth it.

Secret 65

Prepare a Thorough "Scope of Work"

Take the inspection report (submitted by your home inspector during escrow), and compile a list of repairs (also known as "*Scope of Work*"). Then do a walk-through with a general contractor and add everything that needs rehab that isn't already on the list. Then walk through the house again, including items you may have missed the first time around. Missing items here will cause delays and possibly cost overruns later. Take your time and do it right. The budget will be thrown into chaos if you miss items at this step.

Now, go back through your inspection checklist and make a list of items you can repair right away. Put new energy-saving bulbs in all the light fixtures. And invest in simple things that will have an immediate effect, like inexpensive lights and plumbing fixtures.

Next, tear out the existing carpeting, linoleum and old flooring. I've replaced the carpets in almost every house I have ever purchased. This is one item that will pay for itself immediately. But don't replace it until the end. Rather tear the carpet out, then repair and renovate the house with the floors bare, paint everything, and then have the new carpet or tiles installed at the end of the project. And do not use expensive carpet. Use remnants that are low-pile with neutral earth-tones. However, use a slightly thicker pad than normal because it will make the carpet last longer and feels better to prospective buyers walking through the house. If you do happen to get a house with relatively new carpet, have it professionally steam cleaned. (But it's doubtful you'll find many houses that have carpet worth saving.)

Here are repairs you should spend your time and dollars on first:

- Painting
- Carpeting
- Kitchen
- Bathrooms
- Electrical fixtures, including outlets and switches
- Plumbing fixtures and faucets

As you can see, these are all visual items. These will have the greatest impact on your prospects, and the best return on your dollars.

How about items that aren't visual? This will depend on your flipping strategy. If your plan is long-term, you might repair items just to avoid maintenance issues in the future. On the other hand, if you're immediately flipping the house, you might not fix items that are visually and operationally acceptable. An example of a repair you probably wouldn't make would be the inspector's recommendation to replace the old plumbing with cooper pipes. If you plan on flipping quickly, this is a repair that would not add value, and would subtract from profit. So leave it alone.

Secret 66

Rehab With Quality But Less Expensive Items

If you are going to flip a house quickly, rehab using less expensive air-conditioning, heating, plumbing, equipment, and fixtures. But "less expensive" does not necessarily mean less quality. Less expensive may not be about quality issues, but rather simply shorter warranties or an unknown brand. In other words, spend your dollars at Home Depot rather than Lowe's. At any rate, the upfront costs should take precedence over considerations about length of life, extended warranties, or name brands.

Your renovations must be based on your available funds. So calculate a budget and stick to it! If you've had a renovation plan since the beginning, then you likely have already planned on certain expenditures for bringing the house to a saleable condition. At any rate, arrive at an amount that you intend to spend on the project.

The biggest mistake new flippers make is over-improving a house! Here's a huge tip for you: don't over-improve! Let me say it again so it really sinks in: Don't over-improve! It is a waste of your time and money. If an improvement will not increase the selling price, then it probably should be dropped from your list. Let the next owner do it. There are hundreds of resources, contractor cost estimate books, and websites to help you in comparing cost-to-value of improvements:

>www.building-cost.net
>www.get-a-quote.net
>www.ebuild.com

If your goal is immediate resale, then you want to minimize the time between the day you bought the house and the day you flip the house. After all, every day you hold the house you incur costs for taxes, insurance, and utilities. Plus, if you are doing an extensive remodel, there may be additional costs associated with the project. Getting it all done as quickly as possible will cut holding costs, every dollar going back to profit.

Keep colors neutral. Nobody wants blue walls, gold countertops, and orange shag carpeting. No matter what you like, or how cheap the sale was at the discount store, these types of schemes become a distraction. I once bought a house that had been owned by a professional soccer player. Everything in the house was done in bright primary colors. I needed sunglasses just to get past the front door! Don't get creative, leave that for the next owner. As you think about the finished product, just keep in mind beige and off-white. Not that you can't use another color, just don't overdo it. You might think it's cool, but you're not going to live there. For best effect, kitchens should be off-white with a slight tint of yellow. Use bright white, flat latex paint for the ceilings, and semi-gloss for the door frames and baseboards.

Secret 67

Double-Check Estimates and Bids for Accuracy

Always remember that estimates are exactly that ... estimates. When you're calling in contractors to give estimates, always give yourself a little padding to cover their errors (or yours) in defining the scope of the work. The more details you tell them, the better the estimates will be. Contact more than one contractor, and get written estimates based upon your scope of work, not theirs.

Unless there is a huge difference, take the higher one to use as an estimate for this step in your plan. Don't necessarily use the lowest bid for work. You may want it done inexpensively, but you want it done right and on time. There is repair estimate software available for free at many of the major lumber and home improvement centers. Check at their Contractors' Desk. There are also many online repair estimate resources and software programs, such as www.remodeling.hw.net.

Contractor websites have approximate costs for major renovations and improvements. In most localities, there is a contractor or two with more localized estimates for repairs or renovations, usually on their website. For repairs to major appliances, heating, air conditioning, and plumbing, there are many flat rate contractors who can give you firm quotes for work over the phone.

Don't be afraid to also check out the major home improvement stores (i.e. Home Depot, Lowes, Lumber Liquidators) and their websites for estimates. Plus, they usually have contractors available for subcontracting work for their customers and can quickly get you a competitive bid. You can also save money by negotiating a contract where you provide all the materials and they provide the labor. This will allow you to shop for the best value on fixtures, or find discounts on model overruns.

Try to get everything you can as a *"hard bid,"* rather than simply an *"estimate."* This is more likely if the job is simple in nature, or if your specifications are clearly defined. Whether an estimate or a hard bid, get them in writing, with clear descriptions of what they will accomplish for payment. For example, "*Install countertops*" is not sufficient. You need more details. What materials, measurements, how will they be trimmed, and so on?

Secret 68

Monitor Your Contractors Closely

If you're reading this book, you're probably planning on flipping frequently in the future. For that reason, you'll want to maintain good relationships with laborers, contractors, and vendors. Try not to over use their bidding services without giving them a job now and then. If you don't do this, you may find it difficult to get an estimate in the future.

Should you hire handyman types or contractors? There is nothing negative about a handyman. Generally, these are single person or family operations, but you still need to get references and check insurance and licenses. Also, determine whether they have the equipment and resources for your project. The larger the project, the more likely it is that you should work with more established and larger contractors. It could make a big difference with on-time completion and reduced holding costs. Don't even consider using a general contractor unless there are major renovations being done involving at least several subcontractors. Then you know you'll need help. If you're looking for good contractors in your area, checkout these websites:

www.ImproveNet.com
www.ServiceMagic.com
www.AngiesList.com
www.1800contractor.com
www.Contractors.com

Ask all contractors for a copy of their license and proof of insurance. If there's ever a problem, you will need this information for filing a complaint or claim. If they give you excuses about providing it, it will be your first clue that something is wrong. Always confirm that they are licensed, bonded, and insured, or you could end up blowing all your profits in corrective actions, without any recourse.

If it's not in writing, expect things to change, usually to your detriment. There are contracts available online and in office supply stores. If the contractor has his own contract, read it carefully, and feel free to make changes or additions to cover your concerns. You probably don't need an attorney for this.

I have found that many headaches can be avoided by simply listening to your gut. If the contractor is spitting on your living room floor, you probably should pass on him. Common sense can go a long way.

Secret 69

Confirm Your Contractors are Insured

If you are dealing with a general contractor who is hiring sub-contractors, you will need to use *"lien releases."* A lien release is a written document signed by a sub-contractor confirming that he has been paid and is thereby releasing any lien rights he may have. Check the lien laws in your state to see what powers the sub-contractors or suppliers have in placing liens against your house. Have clear payment clauses in your contract and require lien releases from all subs involved before they get final payment. You don't want to finish the project and put up a for sale sign, only to find a lien recorded against your house. By the way, charges for work done in a licensed profession by an unlicensed contractor cannot be liened.

Require proof of liability and worker's compensation insurance from all contractors on the job. Otherwise, you could find a lien recorded against your house in the future due to a claim of on-the-job injury by one of their employees. Keep a file of these insurance certificates with your file of lien releases.

Don't assume that hiring a general contractor who is insured and uses lien releases will take you off the hook for supervision of the project. You must become the supervisor of the supervisor. But if you are acting as your own general contractor, and you're hiring multiple sub-contractors, your job becomes a lot more complicated. There is a lot of coordination required among the building trades in a rehab project. Imagine the problems (and extra costs) if you let the drywall contractor close in the walls before the electrician or plumber finishes his work? Take my word for it, it isn't cheap.

The important consideration for supervision involves your knowledge and abilities. If you aren't sure that you have the knowledge and the time to supervise, or coordinate contractors, hire someone who is suited for the job. Trust me; you'll save money in the end.

Secret 70

Peg Payments to Job Completion Milestones

Whether you're doing one contract with a general contractor, or multiple agreements with several sub-contractors, each document should set out a schedule for each phase of the work and a definite completion date. This is important because each sub-contractor may be dependent on the work of another. You need to be sure that all of those involved at least know your drop-dead date for completion. Plus, there should be contractual penalties for delays that are the fault of the contractor. The more critical your timeline needs, the greater the penalties. Financial penalties work like a charm. You'd be surprised how efficient workers become when they know "late equals a smaller check."

Your best strategy is to peg payments to performance or job completion milestones, but never dates. The problem with structuring payments to coincide with specific dates occurs when the work isn't completed and the date arrives. What do you do then? To avoid this problem, always tie the payments to construction milestones. An example would be breaking down the payments tied to observable completion items. For example, you can make a progress payment based on the completion of all wiring, and then another payment when the walls are completed. In this way, you'll have definite and easily observed checkpoints when payments should be made.

To keep really good contractors happy, and you at the top of their priority list, every once in a while you should pay them a separate bonus for doing a good job and getting work done ahead of schedule. You can even pass out $50 bills directly to workers as a tip. It pays in the long run to keep your best contractors and workers in a good mood!

As the job moves forward, a logically arranged flow chart will keep everyone on track, with deadlines and payments keyed to the items on the chart. Again, money is the greatest motivator.

Are you capable of determining the quality of a contractor's work? Most of us can do an okay job in this area. However, if you're in doubt as to whether a certain job is satisfactory or if equipment was properly installed, pay for another expert to come in and tell you.
Make at least one inspection daily of the project because you can't look inside a wall that's been closed to determine whether the wiring and plumbing were correctly installed. Get your contractors and subs conditioned to the fact that you will not release payments until you have personally walked the job and checked the quality of their work for which they want payment. This sets the tone for the job, and they'll learn that you will not release money unless the work is done right.

Make sure to ask for copies of all building permits that were applied for by the contractor, as well as any final inspection reports from the building inspector.

Secret 71

Use Retentions Judiciously

The amount of money to be withheld from each contractor (*"retention"*) will be based on you signing-off on the satisfactory completion of their job. A typical retention is ten percent. For example, if a contractor is hired for a job at $1,000, then progress payments can be made through the job, but $100 would be held back until you can confirm that the job was completed satisfactorily. This is usually done by holding back ten percent of each project phase or draw. For example, a total job of $25,000, even if there have been multiple draws against the work, would see $2,500 retention when the contractor asks for final completion payment.

Use a *"punch list"* on a final walk-through with a contractor to compile items that need to be completed before the retention will be released. Once the punch list completed, and you are satisfied with the finished product, pay the contractors right away. Your reputation is everything, and word will spread like wildfire throughout the contractor community if you screw around with their money.

When releasing final payment to any contractor, request a signed lien release from them. You will need it for the title company if you flip the house within six months. If dealing with a general contractor, also demand one from all subs and get a signed sworn statement that details all the costs and payments.

Secret 72

Don't Over-Improve the House

One of the biggest mistakes new flippers make is to spend money over-improving a house. This is *"pride of ownership"* taken to the extreme. It is a difficult lesson when a flipper discovers that money spent renovating a property does not always increase the value of that property dollar-for-dollar when flipped. In actuality, the increase in value depends on the kinds of improvements and whether they are commensurate with other houses in the neighborhood.

Here's the secret: Rehab a home to bring it up to (or slightly above) market standards in the neighborhood, but don't exceed those standards. That's why you should spend time checking out the neighborhood and becoming an expert in that area. If you're not sure what improvements will make a real difference, ask your real estate agent for advice. But avoid any temptation to over-improve.

Your goal should be to eliminate anything in the house that is undesirable or unsightly. The house doesn't need to be the best home in the neighborhood. But it should be clean, in good shape, and show well. Some prospective buyers merely take a cursory glance at the property, while others will check everything. Ensuring the little things are in great shape inspires confidence in homebuyers.

You want to make the house attractive to buyers. A clean, attractive house in good repair sells more easily, because buyers can visualize themselves living there. In addition, they can move in immediately without sinking a lot of time and effort into costly repairs and renovations. An attractive house is clean, well-maintained, and has good curb appeal. Here are some suggestions you should consider when rehabbing:

Visual improvements. Perform only fix-ups or improvements that are visible. Painting, installing new carpet, refinishing wood floors, and installing new bathroom fixtures adds real, visible value to a house. But adding extra insulation to an attic will not. Buyers may appreciate your energy-saving gesture (if they even notice it), but they'll never pay a higher price for your efforts.

Structural work. Stay away from structural work if you can. Costs can easily get out of hand as soon as you start modifying the structure. The easiest and most profitable fix-ups are ones that don't require major structural changes. For example, avoid moving kitchen and bathroom plumbing, opening up load-bearing walls, or adding rooms outside the original footprint of the home.

Roof. You want the house to be in good repair, but buyers don't expect perfection. Say you bought a house at a foreclosure auction. The shingle roof is about 10 years old.

The shingles are slightly faded, but no torn or cracked shingles are evident. Still, you're convinced you can increase the curb appeal by replacing the roof. That's a bad idea. The average roof lasts for at least 15 years, and since in this case there are no signs of damage, the roof should easily pass a home inspection. Depending on the size of the house, you could spend anywhere from $5,000 to $10,000 replacing the roof. But here's the problem; a buyer will never pay a premium for a brand-new roof. It might look more attractive, but the house won't sell for a higher price. Giving the buyers a new roof in this case would be like digging into your pocket, pulling out $5,000 to $10,000, and handing it to the buyers.

Luxury Items. Items like wine cellars, dedicated gyms, tennis courts, and swimming pools seldom yield anything close to a good return on investment. The only exceptions would be those amenities that are the norm in the neighborhood and buyers expect them. Even so, the expense is seldom recoverable. For example, you could spend $50,000 installing a swimming pool, yet that adds only $10,000 to the sale price of the home.

Kitchens & Bathrooms. Improvements to kitchens and bathrooms will usually cost more, but will also pay back the most. They're the two types of rooms that buyers look at the most critically. Even buyers on tight budgets want the best possible kitchen and bathrooms they can afford. So plan on spending money on rehabbing the kitchen and bathrooms.

The upgrades in a kitchen can range from basic cosmetics like paint, tile flooring, and stainless steel appliances to expanding the kitchen into an adjoining room. But, it could also include replacing everything from the ceiling to the floor and all the cabinets and appliances.

But don't go overboard! Don't spend $50,000 on granite countertops, tile floors, high-end faucets and fixtures, and a Sub-Zero built-in refrigerator-freezer. That doesn't make sense when every other house in the neighborhood has Formica countertops, standard fixtures, and linoleum floors. Yours will certainly make a splash, but no one will pay a premium for the renovations you've made.

Bathrooms. In bathrooms, the upgrades can be as basic as new fixtures or as extensive as demolishing and rebuilding with a new bathtub, shower, vanity, countertop, tile, and lighting. If the neighborhood supports a luxury bathroom, you may be able to rationalize the expense. Still, do some research and find out if comparable properties featuring high-end upgrades will sell for prices that cover the cost of significant renovations.

Even buyers of a two-bedroom home expect at least a full bath and a half bath to solve the crunch when everyone is getting ready for work and school in the morning. So if you can turn a one-bathroom house into a two-bathroom house by using existing space, you'll likely recover your investment. Similarly, if you can convert a 2-bedroom house into a 3-bedroom house, you will create added value when you flip.

Here's another secret: Whatever repairs, renovations, or improvements you plan to make, be sure they comply with local building-code requirements. Violations can easily give potential buyers second thoughts about the house, not to mention a legal reason to back out of a contract.

Secret 73

Don't Make the Repairs and Renovations Yourself
Unless You Have the Time and Skills

Sure, the more work you do yourself when rehabbing, the more money you'll save. But not if you don't have time to actually do the work and the skills to do it well. After all, if you're already extremely busy, handling repairs and renovations on your own probably doesn't make good financial sense.

In addition, if the repairs and renovations are not up to neighborhood standards, it will cause potential buyers to wonder what else might be wrong with the house. After all, when you're flipping, your goal is to attract as many potential buyers as possible, not scare them away with shoddy craftsmanship. If you don't have the skills to do the work right, either invest time in gaining those skills or hire someone else.

Let's use a simple example. You've purchased a house and you want to paint the bedroom before you flip it. You determine you can save $300 by not hiring a painter and doing it yourself. You arranged a hard-money loan with a lender, and your monthly payment is $1,000. (You have other holding costs, such as insurance, taxes, utilities, and so on, but we'll limit our consideration to the cost of the hard-money loan for the purposes of this exercise.)

You have the best intentions, but you're incredibly busy and it takes you a couple months to free up the time to paint the bedroom. In that situation, you did manage to save $300, but now you're two months farther down the road and you've spent $2,000 in loan payments. If by having the room painted by a professional you could have sold the house two months sooner, you would have enjoyed a $1,700 return on your $300 investment.

Here are some more construction secrets:

If you don't have the time, hire someone else. If you're evaluating a house for flipping, always include estimates for repairs and renovations. If you need to hire contractors or other skilled labor, simply factor those costs into your evaluation.

If you don't have the skills, hire someone that does. For example, don't try to build a perimeter stone wall if you're not a mason. Hire a licensed masonry. Or, if you have the time, consider taking on small jobs firsts to build your skills. Start with a small patio project, and then grow from there. You may learn a lot by taking on a big job, but the meter will be running while you do, and it's your meter that's running!

Evaluate your per-hour cost. Say you're a lawyer with an hourly rate of $300. You have all the clients you can handle. Would you spend eight hours cutting the grass and trimming trees if you could pay a landscaper $20 an hour while you attend to your clients and bill at $300 per hour? Hire out jobs that make sense. For example, if you have good electrical skills, replace wiring or fixtures to avoid $30-an-hour electrician rates. On the other hand, pay a local teenager $8 an hour to cut grass and clean up the yard.

Factor in holding costs. You can save money doing the work yourself, but the longer it takes you do the work, the higher your holding costs will be. Compare the cost of hiring an expert with the holding costs you stand to save. If you can save money by bringing in the pros, do it!

Factor in the value of time spent with your family and friends. Flipping can be an incredible lifelong pursuit. But don't commit yourself to working 20-hour days at your full-time job and flipping properties. Your family will feel deserted and start to resent your investing activities. And you don't want that! After all, spending time with your family is just as important as fixing and flipping houses, if not more so! Balance your work and your home life, and over the long term you and your family will be much happier.

Here's another secret. If you enjoy finding and flipping properties (that are packed with potential), but you're not so good at rehabbing them, then consider partnering with someone who has the skills you're missing. Just be sure that you have a detailed, written agreement that stipulates all the conditions of your partnership.

Secret 74

Give the House a Final Cleaning

When all of the work has been completed, and all of the contractors have permanently left the site, hire a professional cleaning company to come in and get the place "*sale-ready.*" This is one of the most important expenditures you'll make. This is similar to detailing your car. None of the work in the walls or attic should be visible to the potential buyer. The first impression when they walk in shouldn't be dust on the floors or dirty windows. You want buyers' first impression to be a sparkling newly-renovated home.

Section K: Exit Strategies

Secret 75

Always Have a Contingency Plan

No matter how great the house looks, things could go wrong. If you don't have cash reserves to draw on in case of emergencies, make sure that if something does go wrong, you can still sell the house and earn a profit.

To protect against unexpected expenses, you should evaluate each deal using one or two worst-case scenarios. A worst-case scenario is when you say to yourself, *"What's the worst thing I can reasonably expect to happen?"* Then estimate the cost of fixing it.

Every experienced flipper has a horror story to tell. The house that was trashed by previous owners, unknown termite damage to the floor joists that cost thousands to fix, a heating system that died the day after the house was purchased. An experienced flipper who hasn't been unpleasantly surprised is not, in fact, experienced.

For example, let's say you haven't inspected the interior of a house that you're negotiating to purchase. But you can tell from looking at the house from the outside that it is approximately 1,500 square feet. Your real estate agent determines, based on sales comparables in the neighborhood that you can flip the house for $155,000 after you're finished rehabbing it. Accordingly, you decide to list it for $150,000 so that it will sell quickly. You have already determined that your acquisition costs, holding costs, basic repair costs, and closing costs when you sell (including real estate commission) will add up to $25,000.

Now let's imagine a worst-case scenario. The homeowners, angry with losing their home in foreclosure, tear out the toilets and sinks, and trash the carpets when they vacate. Homeowner's insurance won't cover this type of damage since it's intentional. In this scenario, you ask for cost estimates from a contractor, a plumber, and your local carpet outlet. They estimate your costs will be $20,000. If you can purchase the house for $105,000 and this worst-case scenario occurs, you will breakeven on the deal. (If the worst-case scenario doesn't occur, you earn a $20,000 bonus.)

Another worst-case scenario could involve holding costs. We'll use the same example as above. You determine your holding costs (loan payments, utilities, taxes, insurance, etc.) will be $2,000 per month. You plan to complete all repairs and renovations within 30 days and price the property slightly below market value. You plan on selling it within two months. You estimate you'll hold the property for three months, for total holding costs of $6,000.

But what happens if the house doesn't sell, and you hold it for six additional months? In this scenario, your holding costs increase by $12,000 to a total of $18,000. As a result, when you sell, your profit is only $8,000 (rather than the $20,000 you had hoped for).

Other common scenarios to consider include unexpected repair costs like replacing furnaces, appliances, roofs, delays in evicting homeowners, or the effect of rising interest rates. You should always factor in these scenarios when purchasing a house.

Secret 76

It Doesn't Matter That the Former Owner Couldn't Sell The House

Just because the previous homeowner was unable to sell his house, has no bearing on whether you'll be able to sell it. There were undoubtedly various factors that prohibited the homeowner from successfully selling his home. Regardless, if you plan properly, you can avoid these "mistakes" when it comes time for you to sell the house. Let's explore each of these mistakes separately.

For Sale By Owner. Some homeowners realize, once their home is in default that they're over their heads financially. Instead of waiting for a bad situation to get worse, they may try to sell the house themselves.

Their first mistake was not retaining a Realtor to sell their home. Homeowners often try to cut costs by selling the property themselves. Their reasoning is; why pay a 6% commission to an agent when they can sell it themselves and save the money? Fatal mistake. A good real estate agent can usually sell a home in half the time and for more money than the homeowner. They have access to the

Multiple Listing Service ("MLS") and know how to utilize a successful marketing campaign.

Don't make this mistake when it's your turn to sell the house. Hire a good Realtor. The agent will save you on holding costs and ultimately get you a higher price, more than off-setting her 6% commission. In addition, by delegating the task of selling the house to a Realtor, you have more time to pursue other flipping opportunities.

Realtors. Sometimes the culprit is the real estate agent. Some real estate agents do a better job than others marketing their clients' homes. It's very possible the homeowner's listing agent simply put the home on the Multiple Listing Service and hoped for the best. In contrast, some agents know how to market to potential buyers different types of properties. Some have contacts and built a local network of real estate investors who may be interested in the house. Some, quite simply, will work harder on the seller's behalf. When you get ready to sell, make sure you interview several Realtors and select the one that will most aggressively market your house.

Listing Price. The listing price could have been too high in relation to other comparables in the neighborhood. In all likelihood, the owners tried to sell their home at a premium to help them escape their financial difficulties. Many homeowners assume they can start high and then drop the price if no one is interested, but that strategy often backfires.

In a down market, pricing a house above full market value usually means it will take a relatively long periods to sell. In contrast, houses priced below market value will sell more quickly. Always remember the concept of "ready, willing, and able" buyers. A listing price is simply a reflection of what a homeowner hopes the house will sell for. Its true market value isn't determined until the house actually sells. And it may seem a strange phenomenon, but houses that have been on the market for a long time (due to an unreasonably high listing price) will continue to sit on the market (even after the homeowners dropped the price significantly) because buyers are now leery of that seller and that house.

The secret to successful flipping is to aim for a sales price that puts your house just below market value but still allows you to make a reasonable profit. In that way, you can sell the property relatively quickly and with less risk.

    Repairs. The homeowner neglected simple repairs. Houses with obvious defects are very difficult to sell. For example, torn window screens, broken glass, front doors that won't quite close, and overgrown shrubbery are problematic. These houses make a terrible first impression. "*Curb appeal*," the first impression the home makes when potential buyers drive up, is absolutely critical. So, when your time comes to sell, be sure to spruce-up the front yard landscaping, exterior paint, and clean the porch, front door and windows!

Renovations. Obvious renovations have not been made, which is understandable with a distressed property. Homeowners who are struggling financially aren't able to afford repairs, let alone renovations. Outdated appliances, seventies-style carpeting, and weeds threatening to swallow up the front yard turn off potential buyers. Don't make that mistake! A few thousand dollars spent on visual upgrades can make the difference between a quick flip and a long spell on the market.

Unrealistic Profits. Don't try to make a killing on every deal! Remember, your profits are determined by the price you paid, not by what you sell the property for. In other words, pay the right price and your profits are basically assured. Pay too much, and no effort or further investment will help you make a profit.

In summary, when approaching a potential deal, evaluate each possibility, and focus on setting a realistic purchase price. Once you're the owner, make sensible repairs and renovations. Then, when it comes time to flip, list the house with a good Realtor, and aim for a reasonable profit. In that way, you'll be able to flip the house quickly, avoiding the previous homeowner mistakes.

Secret 77

You Can Sell A House Without Completing Renovations

Actually there are several exit strategies available to you that would avoid completing renovations. For example, you could flip the house *"as is"* without performing any repairs or renovations whatsoever. Or, you could complete only the repairs that are absolutely necessary and then sell the house. Or, finally, you could completely rehab the house and then flip it. Let's explore each of these strategies separately.

1. Wholesaling. If you enjoy the hunt for properties and are good at negotiating deals, you can make money without doing any repairs or renovations at all. Using this exit strategy, you simply track down a house, put it under contract, and then turn around and sell the contract ("assign") to another investor for a profit. Once you establish yourself as a having contracts to flip, you'll have a ready source of flippers eager in taking wholesale properties off your hands. And, you'll spend very little, if any, of your own cash!

The process of finding properties and quickly reselling them to other flippers is called *"wholesaling."* The advantages of wholesaling are simple: 1) You don't have to spend time and money performing rehabbing the house; and 2) you'll make money finding great deals for other flippers. The only disadvantages are that: 1) you won't make as much money on each deal, and 2) you could find yourself owning a house that you can't find a flipper to buy.

2. *Repairs Only*. In the alternative, you could make only the repairs that are absolutely necessary. But then, before rehabbing the house, you could flip it to another investor. For example, you find a house in desperate need of cosmetic repairs: paint, carpet, and landscaping. It could also benefit from major renovations, but you don't have the funds. It's the smallest house in the neighborhood, and if you built an addition (i.e. another bedroom and bathroom) you could bring its value in line with the other houses and make a handsome profit when you flip it. The problem is that you only have $15,000 to spend, and you need to flip the house quickly before the holding costs overwhelm you.

In this situation, your best exit strategy might be to invest $10,000 in carpet, paint, and basic landscaping, saving $5,000 for holding costs (or contingencies). Then, when you show the house to an investor, he will see the potential in the property and pay you a premium as a result. In this way, you may be able to double or even triple your $10,000 repair investment.

3. *Partial Rehab*. When doing a quick "down-and-dirty" rehab on a house, you're not transforming it into a showcase home to sell to consumers. Instead, your goal should be to transform the home into a clean, investment property that would appeal to other investors. This means only replacing old or damaged carpet, painting the interior with neutral colors, thoroughly cleaning the entire house, sprucing-up the landscaping, and replacing light fixtures.

Flipping before all of the renovations are completed may reduce your profits, but it will also save you time and keep your investment costs low. In fact, if you have little cash to invest, this might be your only strategy to profit on the deal. Later, when you've built-up your investment funds, you will have more exit strategies to choose from.

At this point, you may be asking yourself, where do I find these investors? You can find investors by placing classified ads in your local newspaper. You can also find them by attending local real estate investment clubs. There is no shortage of investors looking to buy properties. Often these people don't know how to find deals or aren't willing to do the work necessary to find them. Some are part-time investors who hold full-time jobs. Others are brand new. They have cash to invest and resources to rehab a property. Some want to flip the house, while others are looking for long-term rental properties. Regardless, these investors don't have time to find properties, evaluate opportunities, negotiate deals, or rehab properties. But you do, so take advantage of it!

The good news for you is that there are always investors looking to buy properties before, during, and after renovations.

Secret 78

Don't Try to Squeeze Extra Profits When You Flip

Trying to make excessive profits can backfire. For every deal where you manage to squeeze an extra $10,000, you'll have five deals where those same efforts cause your house to sit on the market unsold for months.

So don't try to squeeze extra profits out of every deal. Aim to make a good profit and move on to the next opportunity. Your first goal is to purchase a house as much below market value as possible. Your second goal is to rehab (repair and/or renovate) the house as quickly as possible before holding costs consume your profits. You don't want to spend so much on repairs and renovations that your sales price is out of range in relation to comparable houses in the neighborhood. Your third goal is flip the house quickly for a decent profit.

Keep in mind, you want to offer buyers the best house in the neighborhood at the best price, so it will sell quickly and earn you a good profit. Offering the best house in the neighborhood at the best price means rehabbing the house to bring it in line (or making it slightly more attractive) with other houses currently on the market in the same price range. But what it does not mean is improving the house so extensively that you have to jack-up the price (or wipe out your profit).

To avoid this potential problem, you should develop a plan and budget for repairs and renovations before you purchase a house. Your plan will create a timeline to ensure you complete renovations as quickly as possible, and your budget will keep your spending on track. Basic strategies fall into the four main categories:

1. *No renovations*: Buy a house and flip it to another investor without making any renovations. Many flippers find bargains and simply resell ("assign") them immediately. With this strategy, aim for a $5,000 to $10,000 profit on each deal to start. As you gain experience, you can plan for more.

2. *Quick clean-up*: Find a house in good repair but in need of a thorough cleaning. Clean everything, take care of minor defects, and repair all the systems (i.e. air conditioning, furnace, electrical systems, and plumbing). But don't paint the walls or do any renovations. Price the house below market value, so it will sell quickly. Keep in mind; many buyers enjoy the opportunity to perform their own cosmetic changes to suit their tastes.

3. *Complete rehab*: Clean the house, paint the walls, and perform extensive cosmetic changes (like new carpeting throughout). Also focus on bringing the kitchen and bathrooms up to date, since those are the two rooms buyers will focus on most.

4. *Renovations that add value*: After you've performed a complete rehab, add a new feature(s) to the house. For example, a new patio, a bedroom addition, central heating, air-conditioning, or an extra bathroom will boost the house into a higher price bracket. Your goal is to bring the house up to the standards of the neighborhood. If most of the nearby houses have two bathrooms, adding a bathroom to a one-bathroom house will yield real returns. In contrast, adding a swimming pool to a house in a neighborhood where there aren't any will not add much value to the house.

Remember; your goal is to spend wisely and bring the house up to the comparable standards in the neighborhood. No matter what renovations you make, buyers will almost never pay $300,000 for a house in a neighborhood where the next-best house sells for $250,000. Your goal would be to price your house at $225,000, or possibly $200,000, so that it'll be priced below market and flip quickly.

In some cases, you may be able to add real value to the house. Converting an attic into an extra bedroom or finishing a basement can be relatively inexpensive ways to add value. The key is to determine whether these value-added renovations are worth the time and money you'll spend. To determine whether a feature is worth the expense consider the following:

Check comparables. Determine the value of comparable properties in the neighborhood with the feature you're considering. For example, if you're considering adding a fourth bedroom, check the recent sale prices of four-bedroom homes against the sales prices of three-bedroom homes (all other features considered equal, of course). If you have to spend $15,000 adding a fourth bedroom that will bring a $16,000 return, the reward does not outweigh the risk.

Assess local demand: Visit open houses and talk to real estate agents in the area to learn what local buyers are looking for. Your goal is to make your house attractive to buyers interested in the neighborhood. Find out how much extra buyers are spending for the features your house is missing.

Weigh the cost. No matter what the return, some renovations will be outside your price range. If you have $10,000 budgeted for renovations, considering a $20,000 kitchen makeover is obviously not feasible. Consider other renovations or, if the expected return is high enough, consider borrowing additional funds.

Some flippers actively seek properties with missing features. They pay below market prices for the house, add the missing feature(s) to bring the house in line with other houses in the area, and then flip for a handsome profit. Here are some improvements you can make to add real value to a house:

+ Add a bathroom.
+ Add a bedroom.

+ Add a garage.
+ Replace windows.
+ Replace doors.
+ Add a deck or patio.
+ Convert unused or unfinished space into living space.
+ Add central air-conditioning (if not present).
+ Open the floor plan by converting two small rooms into one larger room.

You can take the same approach, but don't try to make a killing on each transaction. Make a fair profit while reducing your holding costs by getting in and out quickly.

Secret 79

Expect Delays When Flipping Houses

Assuming flipping properties is a way to generate quick cash is a mistake. If you're looking for quick cash, go to the racetrack. If you plan on flipping properties (as opposed to leasing them), you must allow time for delays, unexpected repairs, and a slow sale (especially if the market cools off in your area). If you analyze a deal and the only way to make a profit is to flip the house in less than a month, your risk in all likelihood outweighs the reward. Either find another investor to quickly sell the house to or find another deal.

In addition to the normal delays it takes to rehab a house, list it, and sell it, purchasing properties can also have other types of delays, including the following:

+ Homeowners can take time to make and rethink their decisions.
+ Courts or trustees can delay the process.
+ Homeowners can change their minds at the last minute.
+ The market could cool down and buyers stop buying.

Because of these potential delays, always account for at least two months of holding costs (and more if you can afford it). Even if you perform a minor miracle and can have the house ready in less than 30 days, the house may take as much as two to four months to sell under normal market conditions. And if the market slows, the average amount of time to sell a home can be six months or more. So keep your finger on the pulse of your local market and plan accordingly. Most importantly, never figure on holding a house for fewer than two months.

If there are delays, you will incur holding costs. You can probably expect to pay approximately $100 per day in holding costs. That represents about $3,000 per month. So if it takes at least one month to repair and renovate the house, and another four months to sell it, you need to budget holding costs for five months ($15,000). When you do your calculations, be sure to include these holding costs in your budget. Do the math, and if the deal doesn't make sense, don't do the deal.

Secret 80

Consider all of Your Strategies For Each House

Flipping properties is certainly not the only way to make money. After all, there is no law that says you are required to flip the house after you're finished rehabbing. There are many investors (other than flippers) who buy and hold properties to live in themselves or rent to others. Let's discuss these other exit strategies.

    1. *Your Own Home.* You should always invest in a personal residence for yourself first, before you start flipping houses. Homeownership provides a number of tax advantages. It also lets you benefit from appreciation, and provides you with a place you can proudly call your own. Besides, why pay someone else's mortgage? So, unless you plan to move out of the city in the next year, or a property pops-up that is irresistible (but you don't want to live in), first buy a home for you (and your family) to live in.

    2. *Owner-Occupied During Renovations.* Another strategy is to live in the house while you rehab it. Let's say you buy a house sorely in need of repairs and renovations. You envision the profits you will make when the renovations are completed and the house is flipped. You have the skills to perform the work yourself, or you want to

hire subcontractors to do the work for you. In this situation, you could purchase the house, move in (short-term), and do the renovations at your own pace. Holding costs are no longer an issue, because you're living there! You can take your time, do the work right, save money on the renovations, and increase your profits when you eventually sell.

Plus, using this short-term strategy, you'll enjoy the tax advantages of the *"Personal Residence Exemption."* Pursuant to IRS regulations, if you live in the home, you will be exempt from capital gains taxes when you sell (even if you own more than one home). Here's how it works. If you live in your home for two out of five years, you're exempt from paying capital gains tax, provided you purchase another residence within six months. (If you live in the home for two consecutive years, you qualify. "Two out of five" is used to qualify people who own multiple residences.)

For example, you buy a house for $150,000 and live in it while you spend $40,000 renovating it. At this point, your total costs are $190,000. Four years later, you sell it for $400,000. The $210,000 profit ($400,000 - $190,000) you make is exempt from taxes. You pay no taxes on that profit ("gain") provided you purchase another house within six months from the date of sale. In fact, you can make up to $250,000 on the transaction (or $500,000 if you're married). Anything over those amounts is taxable.

> **Example**:
> Purchase: $150,000
> Repairs: 40,000
> = $190,000 investment
>
> **Four Years Later**:
> Sale: $400,000
> Investment: - 190,000
> Profits (tax free): $210,000

Even better, you can use the *"personal residence exemption"* over and over again. The tax savings can help you buy more properties and increase your net worth. Some flippers who own multiple properties continue to move into a new personal residence every two or three years just so they can take advantage of the tax exemption.

Admittedly, this isn't an option for all flippers (especially if you have a young family adverse to moving), but it is certainly something to think about when you're considering various strategies.

   3. *Rental Property*. Rather than flipping the house, you could buy a house and rent it out to tenants. When you lease the property to tenants, they pay your mortgage. While that may sound impossible, it happens every day! Your tenants pay you rent, which you in turn use to pay your mortgage. So, in essence, they make your mortgage

payment, and you enjoy the benefits. If you buy a house and rent it to others, the monthly rent payments should cover your mortgage payment, taxes, insurance, and other costs. This is called *"positive cash flow."*

On the other hand, if your rental income does not cover your expenses, then you'll have *"negative cash flow."* You should probably not purchase this type of property unless you can afford the negative cash flow, know how to generate additional rental income, or lower your costs.

There are four advantages to owning rental property:

    1. Your tenants pay off your loan(s).

    2. You can deduct your loan interest payments from your taxable income.

    3. You enjoy positive cash flow by collecting more in rent than you pay for the loan, taxes, insurance, and maintenance.

    4. You increase your net worth as your loan balance decreases and the
    house's value increases.

Conclusion

Secret 80 ½

Learning Never Stops

I can hear you now; how can you have "half" of a secret? What's the gimmick? Well, the answer is easy. There are two reasons this is a half secret. First, because it's slightly different than the other secrets in this book. Second, because quite honestly, I thought if I teased you with a half secret, it would pique your interest and you'd remember it.

What is this half secret? The secret is that learning never stops. That education is an on-going organic process. That, just like everything else valuable in life, if you want to be good at flipping houses, you have to constantly expand and update your knowledge. You've taken the first step to becoming a flipper by reading this book. Don't let it stop here. Allow your learning to continue and your knowledge will grow. There are many ways to continue your investing education, such as reading books, attending seminars, networking, and most importantly, doing deals. Let's explore each of these separately.

Books. The next time you have free time, stop by your local bookstore, library, or go online. You will be pleasantly surprised with all of the books in the real estate section. In fact, there have never been so many books on real estate in general, and flipping in particular. There are also books on financing, leasing, tenants, construction, property management, marketing, short sales, REOs, contracts, lenders, foreclosure, and just about any other real estate topic you can imagine. And for the most part, these books are well written (particularly mine). So, now that you have successfully completed this book, read some of other books and expand your knowledge. You'll be glad you did.

Seminars. Reading is good, but nothing compares to "live" seminars and workshops. There is something very special about a teacher standing in front of a room of students explaining concepts and ideas about your favorite topic. Suddenly the subject comes to life! Learning becomes easier. Not only do you have the opportunity to learn new concepts, but live seminars challenge your knowledge by answering the teacher's questions in real time. You also have the opportunity to ask the teacher questions and get immediate answers to concepts you don't understand. So the next time you hear about a flipping houses seminar in your area, run, don't walk, and grab a seat. It will be very educational!

Networking. You should network with other flippers whenever possible. Not only is it a great opportunity to meet people with similar interests, it's always fun to share *"war stories."* Plus, when you network with other investors you have an opportunity to receive advice and make suggestions to others about flipping. It is also an excellent opportunity to meet realtors, mortgage brokers, contractors, and other professionals available for your Dream Team. In most cities, there are real estate investment clubs which meet monthly and offer great networking opportunities. Take advantage of these meetings and network with other investors and professionals whenever possible.

Deals. As the adage goes, you won't catch any fish if you don't put your hook into the water. Well, this adage is particularly apropos for flipping. You can read all the books, attend all the seminars, and network at all the real estate clubs, but if you never purchase a house and flip it, it will all be for naught. This is no time to get cold feet! Don't procrastinate. Stick your hook into the water now! Start submitting offers and negotiating with homeowners and/or lenders. You'll learn more in ONE deal than months reading books and attending seminars. Remember, the first deal is the hardest. But once you get a couple of deals under your belt, it will be clear sailing ahead.

Now get started! Good luck and happy flipping!

Made in the USA
Columbia, SC
29 February 2020